Print: Fashion, Interiors, Art

Published in 2014 by
Laurence King Publishing Ltd
361–373 City Road
London EC1V 1LR
United Kingdom
Tel: +44 20 7841 6900
Fax: +44 20 7841 6910
E-mail: enquiries@laurenceking.com
www.laurenceking.com

A catalogue record for this book is
available from the British Library

ISBN: 978-1-78067-167-3

Design by Shaz Madani

Printed in China

Jacket illustration: Francesco Simeti,
'Hillside', 2014. Courtesy of the artist,
Francesco Pantaleone Arte Contemporanea,
Palermo, and Francesca Minini, Milan.

Print: Fashion, Interiors, Art

Simon Clarke

Laurence King Publishing

Contents

Introduction

From ancient times to the digital age, people have given expression to their imagination by making prints and patterns on the surfaces that surround them – the clothes they wear, the spaces they inhabit, the art they create. In incremental developments, from block printing to digital printing, the narrative that unfolds through this tradition of design echoes the curiosity and inventiveness of both individuals and societies.

A significant stage in this story was the Industrial Revolution of the eighteenth and nineteenth centuries, a time of pioneering inventions that had a transformative impact on all aspects of society. This period revolutionized the technology of printing, especially for textiles, and was instrumental in the awakening realization of the economic benefits to be gained from design. The creation of the toile de Jouy, which depicts landscape and figures in a single colour on a plain ground, added value to mass production, and its popularity continues to this day. The contemporary revitalization of the style has been led by Glasgow-based designers Timorous Beasties, whose toiles depict urban life, warts and all, in the cities of Glasgow, London and New York.

The Arts and Crafts movement of the late nineteenth century, led by William Morris, represented a reaction against the Industrial Revolution and challenged mass production with quality and craftsmanship. The beliefs held by Morris and his peers are now embedded in heritage brands such as Liberty Art Fabrics, whose understanding of quality and imagination blend perfectly through excellence in manufacturing. Technology was particularly influential for print throughout the twentieth century, especially the impact of low-cost synthetic fabrics on printed textile design.

Today, in the early twenty-first century, a wide variety of printing techniques is used around the world, from the very basic to the most advanced, spanning traditional craft practices, industrialization and digitization. While certain historical and cultural subjects persist in print design, new motifs generated by innovations in photography, computer-aided design and the sciences represent a new wave of creative thinking, and suggest a potentially limitless range of possibilities in print. In the same vein, pattern in print is in a state of flux as digital printing has freed it from the conventional parameters of screen and rotary printing. While symmetry in pattern continues, traditional arrangements are reconfigured and newly interpreted, and asymmetries are frequently found in fashion in the form of engineered print designs. Pattern can be explored more broadly in wall panels, and prints made for corporate and domestic interiors increasingly feature a single image for maximum impact. These developments allow new visual rhythms and juxtapositions in pattern systems, which are in a state of deconstruction and reconstruction with few aesthetic limits. While repeat patterns are still popular, they are universally resolved through the use of computer-aided design.

Colour in print has similarly been liberated by technology, with digital innovation enabling a virtually unlimited palette to be used in a design or artwork. The psychology of colour remains important and the atmospheric, emotional and expressive nature it can convey is at play in contemporary print patterns. Colour is still applied to paper using conventional drawing and painting methods, but increasingly artwork is scanned into the computer before undergoing digital manipulation. Designing purely onscreen is increasingly common, with the results remaining entirely in the virtual world until they are realized as digital prints.

The work featured in this book encompasses a wide variety of substrates, from paper to organic, synthetic and blended fabrics through to non-woven materials such as vinyls. Experimental combinations of textiles with non-textile materials are also featured, such as the encasement of printed textiles between panels of glass in architectural constructions. The range of inks, dyes and foils used to apply motif, pattern and colour on to these substrates is broad. The technology available also allows for the efficient and functional use of printed materials in difficult contexts such as performance sportswear products.

In contemporary design and avant-garde art and craft practice, print in its most literal and broad forms consistently extends the conventional boundaries of the field. Hussein Chalayan's conceptually driven symbolic and narrative-based prints bring an original vision to fashion through his individual interpretations of traditional cultural and contemporary themes. Basso & Brooke is another label redefining fashion print through its hyperreal visions of postmodern life. Maharam Digital Projects has created spectacular large-scale wall installations through collaborations with emerging and established artists, photographers, illustrators, fashion and graphic designers, who are resetting the perception of and relationship between art and design in interior settings. In fine art, Brigitte Zieger and Katja Davar convey feminist and political narratives through digital animations with backdrops and props borrowed from traditional print design to achieve dynamic and original results.

The ambition for this book is to showcase many of the most imaginative contemporary examples of print, used in a range of eclectic applications and settings. The work on show hails from around the world and represents many of the most creative and progressive designers, studios, artists and craftspeople working today in a breadth of styles and practices. While for ease the book is divided into the three sections of fashion, interiors and art, there are in fact recurring patterns and creative and technical interrelationships between these areas. It is notable that a number of the individual designers, studios and artists are active in their use of print across two, or all three, of these fields.

The personalities featured here bring originality and a sharp intellect to their creative practice, which they combine with considerable technical dexterity and ingenuity. The diverse nature of their products captures the Zeitgeist of postmodernism and the digital age. Needless to say, the work showcased here leaves us reflecting with much anticipation on what the future may hold, what science fictions and science facts lie ahead and what relevance, resonance and possibilities they may suggest for print.

Fashion

In the early part of the twenty-first century, a number of leading fashion and textile designers and ateliers are producing fashion prints that push the limits of creativity and extend the boundaries of the field. Here we present a selection of contemporary fashion practitioners who are making a significant contribution with their prints, and explore their ideas, working methods and individual interpretations of the fashion print.

The aim has been to capture the designers' personalities and attitudes, allowing them where possible to provide a personal dimension by discussing the work in their own words. It is a testament to these innovators how significant is the intellectual mindset behind the design process, and how effectively their conceptual notions are translated into dynamic and original fashion statements. It is evident that experimentation in technical processes is consistently underpinned by fundamental principles of art and design to uphold levels of excellence in the quality of design and manufacturing. This is true in the making of both analogue and digitally produced printed garments and accessories, and enables original and exciting ideas to become viable commercial commodities, while simultaneously pushing the limits of fashion.

In this opening section, global icons are showcased alongside emerging designers, providing an eclectic mixture of singular and synthesized historical, cultural and contemporary design visions in print. From Japan, the Issey Miyake studio – ceaseless in its pursuit of originality and quality – is represented through a number of prints, including the Spring/ Summer 2013 collection, which employed the novel technique of double-sided heat-transfer printing using bold block motifs to create unique fabrics and garments. In her 2012 collection Miuccia Prada looked back to the 1950s to capture the essence and atmosphere of the time. The sense of style and atmosphere in these prints is perhaps epitomized in the illustrative humorous patterns depicting hot-rod and muscle cars, which speed rhythmically around the Prada garments in this collection. In stark contrast to the Italian style of Prada is the Ethical Fashion Initiative, a collaboration between the International Trade Centre and the fashion revolutionary Vivienne Westwood, which represents innovation, creativity and commerce in a different way. The project, which is aimed at empowering women in the slum regions of Nairobi, Kenya, produces a fusion of upcycled, printed and embellished Vivienne Westwood bags.

This is where the fashion print has arrived at in terms of ideas, technologies and globalization in the postmodern milieu of late capitalism. It is an exciting place with an array of innovations taking form in both the haute-couture and ready-to-wear markets, as well as in menswear and accessories. What seems certain is that the fashion print is not a passive aesthetic: it is active in enhancing the material world, in raising visual consciousness and acting as a conduit through which to cultivate and nurture change on a variety of social, ethical and political fronts while holding on to its traditions. On this evidence, the future of print in fashion looks to continue on a very positive creative trajectory.

Arthur David

Based in Zurich, Arthur David has built an impressive reputation as an innovative designer of printed textiles for the haute-couture market. His individual outlook and the quality of his design ideas have resulted in collaborations with prestigious fashion companies including Jakob Schlaepfer, Matthew Williamson, Valentino and Ben De Lisi. David is equally accomplished as an artist, and his work has featured in a number of international exhibitions, including one at the House of Artists in Tehran.

Despite a prodigious early talent for classical music, his discovery of books about the architects Le Corbusier, Mies van der Rohe, Frank Lloyd Wright and Jean Prouvé motivated David to study industrial design and textiles rather than music. After his design training he decided to work as an artist, including a period of time spent in Paris. On his return to Zurich he worked in the medium of photography, before shifting his focus to printed textiles.

David applies a different kind of thinking in the design of his prints to that used for his paintings or sculptures. He explains: 'In art, I work conceptually, minimalist and purist in relation to the material. Good art always has something timeless. I work faster in textile design, urban in a way, and of course with a spirit of the times.' In his design process he is intuitive, spontaneous and experimental, with reflective moments to enable the final refinement and completion of an idea. He enjoys developing designs that contain graphic and abstract elements, and will work with drawing, painting, paper cuts and photography, finally resolving them in the realm of the computer. The finished designs are then digitally printed on to cloth. Speaking about the development of his designs and

his perspective on fashion, David says: 'I like the option of a rapid intellectual response – pictorially, artistically – in relation to the condition of the world. Fashion is crazy: a mixture of narcissism, vanity and Zeitgeist, between innocence and decadence.'

A key feature of David's digital prints is his manipulation of photography, which is manifested in two forms: first, the creation of staged events, and second, the process of making a photographic print. The first scenario is reminiscent of the choreographed photography of Jeff Wall, with a hint of influence from the artist Gerhard Richter. In these prints David delves into the darker side of human nature, creating staged black-and-white photographs capturing night-time criminal street scenes, dramas played out with the help of his friends. The prints echo certain social anxieties; as David points out: 'in the movies you watch this, but often in reality you will look away.'

David's exploration of the photographic process to generate original designs is reminiscent of techniques employed by Man Ray. In one piece David works with the negative image of a ball of string in front of a projected background. The idea of pattern or repeat is of no interest to him in his photographic prints: they are engineered prints, which can be subsequently worked into repeats by others if desired. This way of working echoes the fact that David does not like the idea of a 'pure' textile, preferring instead to harness the potential of new computer software technology and the opportunities to be found within the field of digital printing. He also generates other types of photographic imagery, such as manipulated materials and fabrics or photographic experiments with crumpled gold and silver foil.

David's design influences arise from a number of places: African cultures are one recurring source of visual inspiration. He is interested in the contemporary art scene and in music, particularly because of his early talents in that area. On inspiration, David says: 'Eccentric and especially narcissistic humans are simultaneously attractive and repulsive. The contradictory is always fascinating. These people invent a very unique aesthetic expression in their clothes and houses, etc.'

A significant feature of David's work is that none of his designs is titled (although they may be numbered). Also interesting is the labelling and marketing of his digital prints: each sample is referred to as a 'panneau', from the French word for a panel, web or sheet of fabric in a specific size or length; the dimensions of each sample are always provided by David alongside this word. He explains: 'I work mostly with sizes 120–140cm wide and 150cm in length (Body length – for example, a long dress/evening dress).' Importantly for the design, this usually means that it has no repeats.

In his design process, David is intuitive, spontaneous and experimental, with reflective moments to enable the final refinement and completion of an idea.

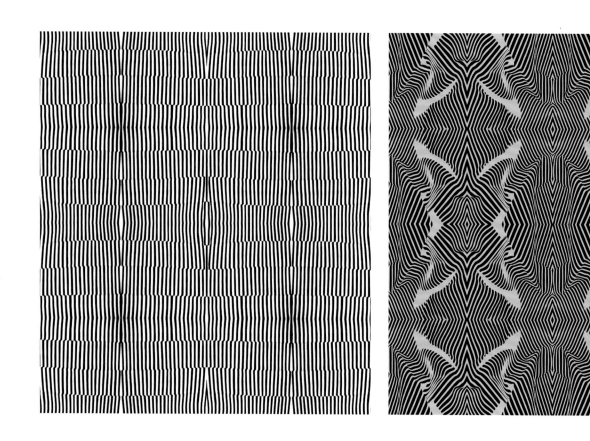

Previous page -- Digitally printed 'panneau' design (W.140cm/L.150cm) for the Ready-to-wear collection, 2013, based on a photographic experiment with crumpled gold and silver foil and projected coloured lights.

Above -- Digitally printed 'panneau' designs (W.120-140cm/L.150cm) for the Ready-to-wear collection, 2013. According to David, the influences for these designs include Op Art and the kilim (a tapestry-woven rug found in North Africa, among other places).

Opposite page -- Digitally printed 'panneau' design (W.120-140cm/L.150cm) for the Couture collection, 2012, based on a photographic design with the negative image of a ball of string in front of a projected background.

Opposite page -- Digitally printed
'panneau' design (W.120-140cm/L.150cm)
for the Couture collection, 2013. Here
David experimented with real fabrics on
the computer to enhance their existing
characteristics and to manipulate them
into patterns.

Top -- Digitally printed 'panneau' design
(W.120-140cm/L.150cm) for the Ready-to-
wear collection, 2011.

Bottom -- Digitally printed 'panneau'
design (W.120-140cm/L.150cm) for the
Couture collection, 2012. For this design,
David worked with colour planes and
projections, partially in motion.

Above and right -- Digitally printed
'panneau' designs (W.120-140cm/L.150cm)
for the Ready-to-wear collection, 2013,
based on still photographs, taken by the
designer, of a street crime scene staged
by David's friends.

Opposite page -- Digitally printed
'panneau' design (W.120-140cm/L.150cm)
for the Couture collection, 2011, based
on a staged still photograph, taken by
the designer, of two flower heads before
a projected background, reduced to black
and white and lightly coloured.

Basso & Brooke

The design team of Bruno Basso, graphic artist, and Christopher Brooke, garment architect, has redefined fashion through an inimitable vision. Original conceptual thinking, experimental digital prints, inspired tailoring and a desire to evolve render this a design label with a unique approach.

Innovation in design and production has always been characteristic of Basso & Brooke's work. The early collections were inspired by sources as diverse as the writers H.G. Wells and Jules Verne, traditional Japanese iconography and a postmodern aesthetic reminiscent of the styling in Ridley Scott's film *Blade Runner* (1982).

Visionaries in the field of art and design and from other disciplines inform Basso & Brooke's thinking and underpin their ideals. The African explorer David Livingstone is quoted in one press release: 'I am prepared to go anywhere, provided it be forward.' While this quotation is historical, the collection in question is progressive, echoing such hyperrealistic sources as the paintings of Jeff Koons and the black-and-white nude photography of Herb Ritts.

Basso & Brooke's eclectic design process produces work that reflects the duo's creative dexterity. This is evident in the Autumn/Winter 2011–12 collection, inspired by the iconic 1960s fashion model Veruschka and the make-up artist Holger Trülzsch. The critic Susan Sontag's introduction to the book *Veruschka: Transfigurations* (1986) captures the essence of this collection's aspiration: 'What a compendium of desires – contrasting, contradictory; impacted, immobilizing. The desire to escape from a merely human appearance: to be an animal, not a person, an object (stone? wood? metal? cloth?), not a person; to be done with personhood

… The desire to be emblematic, to become image; artifact; art; form … The desire to become fully visible, to be seen … The desire to hide, to be camouflaged.'

Working with natural, classic and less conventional ideas about camouflage, the digital prints in Basso & Brooke's Autumn/Winter 2011–12 collection present the viewer with oxidizing metal, peeling paint and crumbling concrete, in large scale and in fragments and fused with flashes of birds. The prints feature abstract blurring similar to that seen in the paintings of Gerhard Richter, removing excessive detail and resulting in enigmatic camouflage. Fashion forms draw on classic and modern shapes to begin with, but transform little by little into declarations of Bohemianism.

Basso and Brooke pooled new experiences to create the digital prints and fashion forms of the Spring/Summer 2012 collection. For Basso, an expedition by car from London to Beijing, driving for weeks through a bleak and brutal landscape in the Siberian twilight, became an assimilated visual resource and the impetus for the design of these prints; hard, angular lines, sharp contrasts and strong structures feature – the essence of Constructivism. To counter the hard-edged graphic, Basso adds alien moments of colour, creating what he calls 'tropical Constructivism'. Hard-edged foliage collides with distorted seascapes, and man-made textures explode over fading sunlight.

During the design process for this collection, a second idea emerged, the very notion of the definition of 'a collection'. Instead of producing a range of prints, why not let them evolve from one garment to the next? For Brooke, a journey into drapery transforms the graphic prints into moving three-dimensional forms. In other instances, the

printed *trompe-l'œil* effect becomes emphasized by Brooke's tailoring skill to create further spatial play. Basso & Brooke's aspiration to evolve is noted in this season's press release, which includes a quotation by the artist Robert Rauschenberg: 'It's when you've found out how to do certain things, that it's time to stop doing them, because what's missing is that you're not including the risk.'

The French painter Henri Matisse inspired the direction for the Autumn/Winter 2012–13 collection, both through his innovative paper cuts and by way of his personality, his desire and confidence to set aside his own rule book and approach his work from a new angle. 'This represents a new phase in our work,' says Basso. As with Matisse's paper cuts, the prints in this collection are fairly simple, flat and graphic, but they contain iconic and familiar patterns from every era. The effect is a Japanese aesthetic that is occasionally – and surprisingly – juxtaposed with unusual experiments with perspective that suggest impossible geological strata and splashes of iridescent elements seen under a microscope. The garments feature exaggerated details, and masculine and feminine leanings are given equal weight. 'The way we worked with the prints this season gave us lots more room to experiment with the way we constructed the garments,' says Brooke.

Previous page -- 'Far From Home'
(detail), Spring/Summer 2012. Inspired
by Basso's road trip, this asymmetrical
design for a digital print incorporates
landscape, a photographic crowd scene,
geometric blocks of colour and foliage.

Above and opposite page -- 'Tippi',
Autumn/Winter 2011–12. Peeling wall
textures, birds' wings and photographic
portraits of the actress Tippi Hedren
in Alfred Hitchcock's 1963 film *The Birds*
make up this engineered digital print.

To counter the hard-edged graphic, Basso adds alien moments of colour, creating what he calls 'tropical Constructivism'. Hard-edged foliage collides with distorted seascapes, and man-made textures explode over fading sunlight.

Above left -- 'Tropical Constructivism',
digital print with hard-edged foliage
and fading sunlight. Spring/Summer 2012.

Above centre -- Seascapes, foliage and
line drawings combine to create this
asymmetrical digital print on a loosely
structured garment. Spring/Summer 2012.

Above right -- Photography and a fluid,
abstract orange motif make up this
digital print set within a fluidly
tailored garment. Spring/Summer 2012.

Opposite page -- 'Disintegrated Sky',
digital print, Spring/Summer 2012.
Golden and embroidered fabrics create
mirror-image seascapes and futuristic
constructions in this design.

Opposite page and above left -- These eclectic digital prints fuse the paper-cut magic of Henri Matisse with Japanese aesthetics and patterns reminiscent of geological strata. Autumn/Winter 2012-13.

Above centre -- The juxtaposition of patterns and colours within a strong vertical composition generates rhythm and movement. Autumn/Winter 2012-13.

Above right -- With innovative garment construction, the reinvention of the evening dress as canvas has a great impact through the bold decorative elements in the digital print. Autumn/ Winter 2012-13.

Dries Van Noten

Dries Van Noten first presented a menswear collection in London in 1986, as part of the 'Antwerp Six' collective. Since then he has become a recognized innovator in fashion, with prints playing an important role in the originality of each new collection. Now based in the dockland area of Antwerp, he produces four ready-to-wear collections each year. He has become recognized as a cerebral designer, which becomes evident when he outlines the source of the creative triggers for his new collections: 'One season I'm inspired by a picture, the next by a complete exhibition. It is more an evolution in the mind than a fixed process; things grow over the years. Sometimes recent things – images, a book – … can have an impact on a collection; sometimes it is only years later that you remember something you saw without really paying attention to it. There are also things or colours that I don't like or that I think are ugly, and I force myself to discover why I think those things are ugly or why I don't like them. This journey brings you to another approach towards these things.'

For the Autumn/Winter 2011–12 collection, inspiration came from a fictive encounter between Ziggy Stardust and the Ballets Russes, a concept that reflects Van Noten's interest in the convergence of different ideas. It was realized through patchworking contrasting and conflicting woollen and silk fabrics with vibrant colours and prints to asymmetrical garments. Van Noten explains: 'We really didn't choose the prints for any technical aspects, we just wanted to choose varying options depending on how they either clashed or fused with those to which they were connected.'

Van Noten has been inspired by many different artists, including Francis Bacon, Robert Mapplethorpe and the Belgian Jef Verheyen. The Mexican artist Gabriel Orozco was an influence on the Spring/Summer 2012 collection. Van Noten explains why: 'In his works made by cutting up the phone book into strips and covering a wall with just the telephone numbers, I found that he took art out of the studio. I liked that it was so eclectic, that it goes in all directions. A painting, a photograph, an installation … all that I love. It inspired us to use etchings, pictures and publicity photos, and to make prints from elements that were never meant for fabrics.' Another influence on this collection is the Marseille-based British photographer James Reeve, with whom Van Noten collaborated, applying Reeve's night cityscapes to printed textiles.

Van Noten works with different print media each season, using whatever is best suited to what he is designing, be it hand screen-printing or digital printing. In the former, the colour penetrates the fabric better and gives what Van Noten calls a more 'authentic' look. However, he recognizes the potential of digital prints: 'The possibilities and ways of working with digital prints are endless, and it's a quicker and more flexible process.' He has no preferences, and likes to play with the contrast between varying possibilities. 'The same motif printed on a cotton or on a silk shantung will always give you a completely different result, and in a way the method in which you print will give more character to the piece,' he says.

In each collection, Van Noten strives to be innovative in some way, and his love of fabrics and print means that these are the aspects of a new collection that he finds both interesting and exciting. 'The research into how to print something … on to a new or delicate fabric, while nerve-wracking and time-consuming, is as fulfilling as anything, in my eyes. One always has to surprise the public, and I also want to surprise myself and challenge my team … not to make ourselves get stuck in a "Dries Van Noten" way of thinking.'

Previous page -- The Autumn/Winter 2011-12 collection is a conceptual blend of elements focusing on the imagined interplay between Ziggy Stardust and the Ballets Russes.

Opposite page, top left -- A wilderness landscape with rapids and towering escarpment from a seventeenth-century monochromatic copperplate etching is transferred to cloth. Spring/Summer 2012.

Opposite page, top right -- This atmospheric engineered print with photographic junglescape in Kelly green is collaged with a monochromatic seventeenth-century copperplate print depicting a pastoral scene. Spring/Summer 2012.

Opposite page, bottom left -- Black-and-white floral motifs combine with coloured botanical etchings on an optic white ground to form this photomontage. Spring/Summer 2012.

Opposite page, bottom right -- This print features a monochromatic copperplate etching alongside a seascape and a night cityscape. Spring/Summer 2012.

Right -- This engineered print brings together vivid details of seascapes and butterfly wings, which are combined with a large-scale centre-piece showing a scene from the seventeenth century using the copperplate print technique. Spring/Summer 2012.

'One season I'm inspired by a picture, the next one by a complete exhibition. It is more an evolution in the mind than a fixed process ...'

Opposite page -- Inspiration for this print is drawn from *ukiyo-e* ('pictures of the floating world'), a genre of Japanese woodblock prints and paintings that rose to popularity in the second half of the seventeenth century. Autumn/Winter 2012-13.

Above left -- In this garment, dynamic panels of blue contrast with embroidered details. A flavour of the military costume permeates through, as do the codes of a bourgeois wardrobe. Autumn/Winter 2012-13.

Above centre -- While oriental in design, this uniquely composed engineered print is transformed into a contemporary abstract, with suggestions of Op Art echoing through the use of acid pastel colours. Autumn/ Winter 2012-13.

Above right -- This garment captures the magic of print design with virtual pleating, whereby shards of print photographed on one garment are repeated on another to replicate pleats. This aesthetic is blended with ethnic patterns in contemporary abstract compositions. Autumn/Winter 2012-13.

Opposite page -- A bold print pattern
is inspired by the illustrative
and calligraphic style of the Dutch
contemporary designer Job Wouters.
Autumn/Winter 2012-13 menswear collection.

Right -- This elegant psychedelic print
and garment evokes a bizarre conceptual
collision between Oscar Wilde and Frank
Zappa. The print is informed by the
mural paintings of Gijs Frieling. Autumn/
Winter 2012-13 menswear collection.

Heidi Chisholm and Shine Shine

After studying graphic design, Heidi Chisholm co-owned a design agency in Cape Town that drew on Africa as its inspiration. African aesthetics and experiences continue to influence Chisholm, who was born in South Africa but now lives in New York. She maintains connections with her home country through her client and friend Tracy Rushmere, owner of the company Shine Shine, a studio involved in the creative production of printed textiles.

Although Chisholm's design output for Shine Shine is modest, that means the level of creativity and invention is high. During the design process – an intuitive, 'African' one, Chisholm suggests, with 'Eureka!' moments and few rules – she gathers visual information and makes sketches and notes. In this client-friend relationship, Chisholm and Rushmere have their own ideas about a new design. 'It is not only my ideas that I end up designing,' Chisholm explains. 'Often Tracy will tell me she wants something, and I will go with that and add my own ideas to it.' Once there is agreement, further research and new drawings follow. Drawings are either done on paper and refined on the computer, or made from the outset on the computer.

Chisholm's first design for Shine Shine was 'Julie Juu', influenced by Mexican and Catholic iconography such as the snake and the Virgin Mary, which she became aware of through Mexican shops in Brooklyn. She combined this imagery with the motif of Julie Juu, inspired by photographic portraits by the Malian photographer Seydou Keita. 'The eclectic mix of ideas, inspiration and icons is … a very African thing,' she points out: it is not uncommon to find Catholics in South Africa who also follow the traditional African religion of their forefathers, mediated through *sangomas*, traditional South African diviners. This

blending of Catholic and African religions equally persists in Mexico. Rushmere was keen for the Julie Juu character to be portrayed in this design as a virgin.

The design 'Jackie So' was inspired by a Facebook friend who was obsessed with her boyfriend and with shoes. The 'gorgeous boyfriend', as Chisholm puts it, is inspired by another of Seydou Keita's photographs. Chisholm additionally reveals: 'Actually, the truth is that Tracy has been asking me forever to do a sexy girl with trucks.' In the case of the designs 'Obama' and 'M O Baby', the thinking is different again. 'Obama' evolved from the printed commemorative and political cloths found in a number of African countries, popular during elections. Chisholm explains her motivation: 'An African man becoming President of the United States, and me living in America now – it just felt that every aspect of that shouted to become a fabric.' After the 'Obama' design, Chisholm and Rushmere decided that there should be one for Michelle Obama, which resulted in 'M O Baby'.

As part of the creative discourse with Rushmere, specific motifs developed in a design by Chisholm will be taken out. In the 'Obama' design, for example, Chisholm says: 'I had the American flag as a pattern in the background, and Tracy wanted me to change it to roses, so I did, and it ended up being a very good decision. I had elephants and scissors and little dots in the background of [the] Michelle Obama [design]. Tracy wanted it to stay very graphic, flat, feminine and "sexy", and I took the dots, elephants and scissors out and changed the background to flowers. Tracy has a clear vision for her brand, and she keeps me on track.'

The remarkable 'No. 1 Football Fan' design for the 2010 FIFA World Cup, held in South Africa,

was motivated by Chisholm's husband and the idea to use the football fans as motifs. In South Africa football fans wear bizarre headgear called *makaraba*, adapted from builders' hard hats. The fans cut shapes out of the hats, add additional forms and paint them. The result is a highly decorative, sculptural helmet. The fans also wear enormous glasses, which they make and decorate. They might carry an object in each hand, such as a decorative *vuvuzela* horn. This stunning visual resource led to this innovative design.

African artists such as Chéri Samba and Bodys Isek Kingelez, hand-painted barber-shop signs and African textiles all influence Chisholm's choice of colours. Adjustments to colour are guided by Rushmere, using her experience in selling printed textiles. African textiles are replete with symbolism, and the perception of Shine Shine's customers is that the studio's printed textiles convey meaning. Chisholm likes to push this notion, and does so just enough that the customer feels as though a design has meaning but is not entirely sure, resulting in new meanings being assigned to the designs by the customers. The inclusion of African proverbs is established in African textiles, and Chisholm is playful in combining text with motifs to distort the original meaning of the motif. Some proverbs are politically incorrect or, as Chisholm says, 'might make a feminist jump through the roof', which she finds funny.

Previous page -- 'No. 1 Football Fan',
print designed at the time of the 2010
World Cup, held in South Africa.

Above -- Conceptual artist Kelly
Vaagsland's 'Shack Couture' was a
site-specific piece that involved
wrapping a pink shack in Khayelitsha
Township, Cape Town, in a bolt
of the 'Obama' printed cloth.

Right -- 'Obama' (detail): portrait of
President Obama with the fist of hope and
the text 'Hooray for the President'.

'The eclectic mix of ideas, inspiration and icons is ... a very African thing'

Opposite page -- 'M O Baby', a follow-up
design to 'Obama', portrays Michelle Obama
with accessory motifs and the words 'Don't
Stand in my Light' and 'Never Go To Bed
Without Washing Your Dishes'. The use of text
is a popular feature in African prints.

Above -- 'M O Baby' (detail): the reclining
Michelle Obama in conversation on the
telephone, accompanied by a snow leopard.

Above -- Visual inspiration from an
eclectic range of sources culminated in
the creation of the print 'Julie Juu'.

Opposite page -- The 'Jackie So' print
conveys a simple narrative of obsession.

Hussein Chalayan

Through his conceptual and technological approaches to fashion, Hussein Chalayan is now acknowledged as a creative pioneer, and prints play an important role in his innovation. The originality of thinking in his use of digital print is graphically conveyed by the 'Kaikoku' collection of Autumn/Winter 2011, inspired by Japanese culture and presented as a film. *Kaikoku*, or open country, refers to the period that followed *Sakoku* ('chained country'), when Japan was closed to foreigners. The digital prints in the 'Kaikoku' collection are characterized by the use of shadows; the Japanese recognize that, while an object in itself may not necessarily be beautiful, beauty can occur in the shadows it creates. The concept is echoed in the film, for example by projecting the shadow of an actual window grate on to a print that evokes the shadow of an aeroplane as if seen through a grate. Chalayan explains his thinking behind the collection: 'The idea was to show a working process that leads to the prints by using tools like the aeroplane and window grate in the 'Kaikoku' film. In this film, I demonstrate how these prints came to be. By working on these prints I wanted to symbolize the opening of Japan after the *Sakoku* period.' This collection differs in atmosphere from the preceding 'Sakoku' collection (Spring/Summer 2011), also presented as a film, which featured a performance aspect simulating *bunraku* (traditional Japanese puppeteers) manipulating the fabric of the garments.

A very different perspective prevails in the print pieces in the 'Sip' collection (Spring/Summer 2012): 'The florals were always shifting to symbolize the idea of arts and crafts becoming digitalized.' The prints formed only one aspect of this ingenious collection: when presented on the catwalk, the models appeared to sip from champagne flutes. Tiny wireless cameras inside the flutes lit up when the glasses were tipped, capturing the inside of the models' mouths. The audience was rendered voyeur as the models' lips, teeth and throats were projected in real time on to canvas behind the catwalk.

The 'Domisilent' collection (Autumn/Winter 2012) unfolds as a number of chapters. Particularly interesting for print is the chapter 'Cause and Effect', in which brightly coloured motifs are shown on grey and light grey grounds. Chalayan is keen to emphasize that the key to the prints is in the aesthetic result, rather than in the concept, which he underplays. He drew inspiration for the print motifs from ship parts and bacteria, representing warships and chemical contamination.

The inspiration for the 'Seize the Day' collection (Spring/Summer 2013) is life's ordinary and everyday moments, which are given value and resonance and thereby made more special. Shades of lime green, peach and mint prevail in Chalayan's photographs of his own pile of laundry, printed on to metallic Jacquard in an apparently random way to achieve an astonishingly beautiful aesthetic. The fabric prints are subsequently worked into peplum tops and evening dresses. Other pieces in this collection capture another personal moment observed by Chalayan. In the luxurious environment of a museum, marble statues are contrasted with a utilitarian air vent on the wall. One garment illustrates the concept through a digitally printed black marble column, with the air vent reinterpreted as a thin cut-out rectangle at the front of the garment and highlighted by the use of the luxurious precious metal palladium. Chalayan asks us to conceptualize around this garment, to imagine the spatial, visual and aesthetic tension created when a woman visits a museum in the marble-print dress and finds herself admiring a marble statue.

The 'Sakoku' collection featured a performance aspect simulating *bunraku* (traditional Japanese puppeteers) manipulating the fabric of the garments.

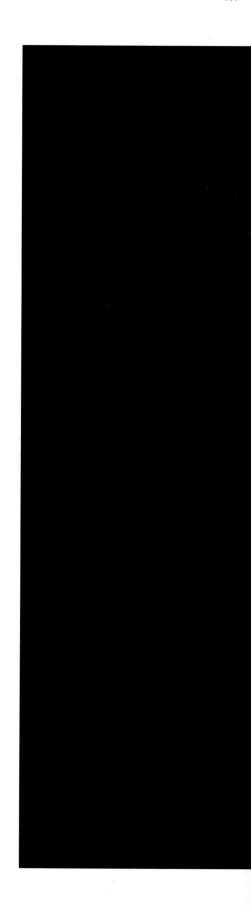

Previous page -- A shadow projection of
an aeroplane as if seen through a window
grate is rendered as a digital print
in the innovative 'Kaikoku' collection,
Autumn/Winter 2011.

Right -- A garment with a floral kimono
print is manipulated by a *bunraku*
puppeteer in the film for the 'Sakoku'
collection, Spring/Summer 2011.

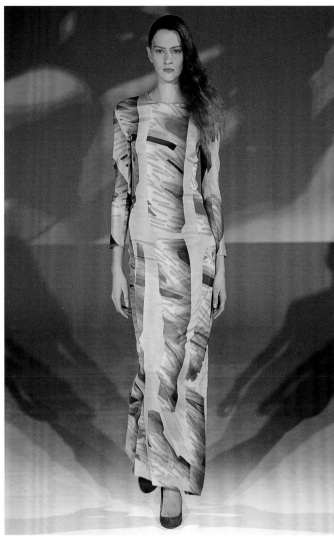

Opposite page -- In the 'Sip' collection,
Spring/Summer 2012, Arts and Crafts-
inspired florals shift to represent their
transference into the digital realm.

Above -- Pieces from the 'Domisilent'
collection, Autumn/Winter 2012. The
inspiration for these digital prints
originates from warships and chemical
contamination. Chalayan aesthetically
transforms the source material with
his consummate design skills, blending
dynamic rhythms and movements with
perfectly balanced rich colours and
neutral grey tonal elements.

Above -- The contents of Chalayan's own
laundry basket are photographed and
printed on to metallic Jacquard fabric
for the 'Seize the Day' collection,
Spring/Summer 2013.

Opposite page -- This piece from the
'Seize the Day' collection, Spring/Summer
2013, evokes a black marble column in a
museum, with a cut-out panel representing
an air vent.

Issey Miyake

This iconic Japanese clothing company has flourished under the creative direction of its founder, Issey Miyake, since its inception in 1970. Miyake's aesthetic and technological vision is the key to the brand's consistent flow of progressive fashion collections. The latest inkjet printing technology is one among many manufacturing techniques he has used to facilitate innovation.

A case in point is the 'Guest Artist Series', in which technology and the conceptual came together to produce new ideas for clothing. Miyake collaborated with various artists, including Yasumasa Morimura, known for his large-format colour self-portraits; Nobuyoshi Araki, renowned for his photography of female nudes and bondage portraits; and Tim Hawkinson, who uses his own body parts and unusual items such as toy eyeballs to create his art. All three artists realized their ideas through the medium of printed textiles in Issey Miyake's 'Pleats Please' range. This technological innovation by Miyake, inspired by Mariano Fortuny's pleated dresses from the 1920s, creates permanent pleats in polyester using heat treatment. Miyake sees 'Pleats Please' as his most important contribution to design yet.

The level of extreme imagination in the 'Guest Artist Series' is exemplified by the fourth guest, Cai Guo-Qiang, the visual director of the Beijing Olympics, whose performance piece involved detonating sprinkled gunpowder in the shape of a dragon on to garments and subsequently printing the scorched traces on to 'Pleats Please' pieces. In an interview for the fashion magazine *Figaro Japan* at the time of the collaboration, Cai said that Miyake is always on the borderline between destruction and creation, so he is constantly creating new worlds. In fact it is fair to say that all the collaborations break

new ground through the fusion of art and fashion. The intention of this series, apart from producing progressive garments, was perhaps more to provoke than to make aspirational art statements.

Over time, Miyake has diversified his research interests. As well as 'Pleats Please', he has created the 'A-POC' (A Piece of Cloth) project, in which a thread becomes a piece of clothing using one piece of machinery. He also played a significant role in the realization of 21 _ 21 Design Sight, the first design museum in Japan. Importantly, he remains a presence at Issey Miyake, where his astute creative thinking permeates.

Yoshiyuki Miyamae is the current creative director of womenswear at Issey Miyake, having previously worked under Miyake and the company's former creative director Dai Fujiwara for ten years. As a consequence of his first-hand experience in Miyake's design studio, Miyamae has naturally assimilated and consequently upholds the design ethos created by Miyake. He does, however, combine it with his own creative vision to ensure the company stays at the forefront of contemporary culture. Miyamae's second collection, for Spring/ Summer 2013, named by him 'Flapping Colours', was inspired by the vibrant, beautiful hues of feathers. Initially manifesting themselves as static motifs, they became a more complex vision of birds flapping their wings as they descend on to water. The silver reflective surface of the catwalk captured the reflections of the prints, and the models criss-crossing the catwalk at the end of the show gave the impression of birds flapping above a lake.

The print designs in the collection were a combination of large, irregular geometric patterns, which were intelligently placed on the garments to create an illusion of depth. The design

motifs were formed of large blocks of bright, vibrant colours – purple, red, yellow, blue and turquoise, among others – which worked alongside or with partial or complete overlays of black-and-white stripes and similarly striking black-and-white patterns. The technique of double-sided heat-transfer printing added significant depth to these pieces. This printing technique combined dramatically with new kinds of pleating and the consequent stretch potential to create a variety of optical effects.

There is more than a hint of influence in these pleated transfer prints from the project '132 5. Issey Miyake', the impetus for which came from the discovery of a digital graphic application that starts with a single plane and mutates it into a three-dimensional model. The number '1' refers to the fact that one piece of cloth can become three-dimensional ('3'), and can be refolded into its two-dimensional ('2') state. The number '5' after the space signifies the temporal dimension that comes into being after the clothing is worn. This pleating technique had a very interesting effect on the heat-transfer printing and on the aesthetic of the subsequent print.

A significant reason for the success of Miyake's design practice is that it functions in an environment where there is the freedom to have ideas. It is not just about the advancement of Miyake's own ideas, however; it is also about the cultivation of skill in the people around him, as in the case of Miyamae. This supportive creative environment is one that retains traditional principles at its core but where design is free to evolve.

Previous page -- Vibrant hues and
innovative pleating techniques merge
in double-sided heat-transfer prints
for the 'Flapping Colours' collection,
Spring/Summer 2013.

Right -- Yoshiyuki Miyamae, creative
director for womenswear at Issey Miyake,
took inspiration from brightly coloured
feathers for the vibrant palette of the
'Flapping Colours' collection, Spring/
Summer 2013.

**The design motifs were formed of
large blocks of bright, vibrant colours –
purple, red, yellow, blue and turquoise – which
worked alongside or with overlays of
black-and-white stripes and similarly striking
black-and-white patterns.**

Above -- Design development sheets for
'Flapping Colours', Spring/Summer 2013.

Opposite page -- Pleat innovation with
double-sided heat-transfer prints,
Spring/Summer 2013. While reflecting
the ethos of the 'Pleats Please' brand,
these pieces mark an evolution through
the introduction of multi-directional
pleating with bold abstract prints.

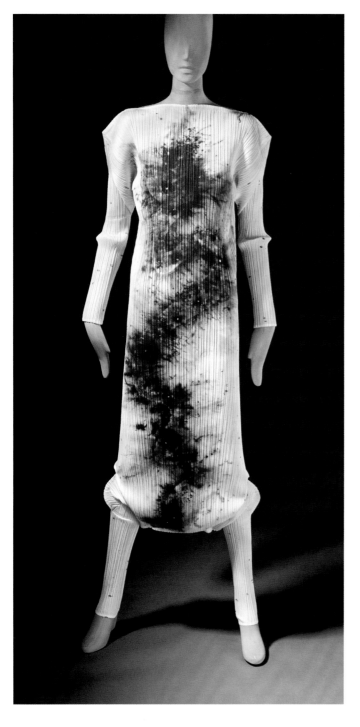

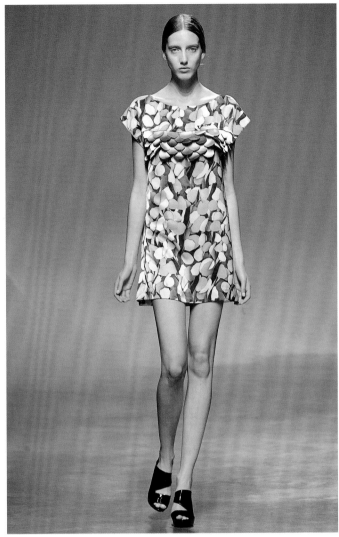

Opposite page -- Jumpsuits designed in
collaboration with Miyake for the 'Pleats
Please Issey Miyake Guest Artist Series':
by Cai Guo-Qiang for the Guest Artist
Series no.4, 1999 (left), and by Tim
Hawkinson for the Guest Artist Series
no.3, 1998 (right).

Above -- Prints designed by former
creative director Dai Fujiwara for the
Spring/Summer 2011 collection 'Ghost
in the Clothes', informed by the ghost
stories of Alfred Hitchcock.

Jakob Schlaepfer

With more than a century of experience in the textile industry, Jakob Schlaepfer, based in St Gallen, Switzerland, has built its success on the manufacture of fine embroidery. This success persists principally because the company has consistently embraced the latest developments in creativity and technology. As a result of this progressive outlook, it has become one of the world's most innovative producers of luxury fabrics for the haute-couture, ready-to-wear and interiors markets.

In a process of creative and technical evolution, Jakob Schlaepfer has diversified, resulting in the emergence of a flourishing print section. Print is not new at the company – it carried out early experiments in multicolour printing in the 1920s – but this ongoing involvement with the technology has contributed to the organization's original, contemporary vision for print. The company embraces the opportunities presented by digital technology, and displays its motivation to move into the future with print by investing in the latest inkjet technology. Such investment results in the production of avant-garde printed textiles, since this digital technology presents significant creative opportunities for extreme, lavish new approaches. It has led to the printing of designs with remarkable levels of invention and acute attention to detail. These new degrees of quality have been achieved through the use of high-resolution photography and macro-scale imagery, resulting in the application of larger-than-life photography to print. Details in paintings translate extremely well through inkjet printing technology and, in combination with photographic elements, are applied to both fashion and interior contexts.

The creative scope of this technology enables the application of phenomenal hyperreal explosions of form and vivid colour to fabric and wallpaper, capitalizing on the ability of computer-aided design to produce complex pictorial montages. Equally significant are painted patterns with cultural references and abstract, expressive motifs in dramatic colours. Excitingly, translating painted imagery through digital printing means that Jakob Schlaepfer is able to capture the essence and integrity of the original artwork on the cloth or wallpaper substrate.

The mindset at the company is without doubt forward-thinking, and this vision is exemplified in the creative director, Martin Leuthold, whose experience and openness to innovation are at the core of the company's continuing competitiveness. This is maintained by pushing the boundaries of creativity, by involving imagination and lateral thinking in the design process while remaining mindful of the fluid state of the clients' markets. Keeping one step ahead is an essential part of the company's philosophy; it is what the design team tirelessly works towards and is adept at. Turning visions into real textiles is the key skill of the design team, and Leuthold – with his know-how and openness to new ideas whatever the source – ensures a highly desirable product of real appeal to clients from around the world. This is backed up by the fact that the company can sell 2,500 designs in a year to leading fashion houses.

It is not only fashion designers who are attracted to Jakob Schlaepfer's inspirational luxury fabrics: architects and interior designers have also responded well. Clients are drawn to the high quality and experimental approach to design and are unsurprisingly of a similar mindset. Leading companies in the fashion industry apply the fabrics of Jakob Schlaepfer to their creations, including Chanel, Vivienne Westwood, Alexander McQueen and Christian Lacroix. This impressive client base is the result in large part of Jakob Schlaepfer's commitment to research and development, and that is one reason the company is in a positive state of flux.

There are, however, other types of client, less visible in terms of profile but significant in their impact, such as a couturier working on exclusive fabrics for the queen of Brunei, as well as – perhaps not surprisingly – such other clients as Disney and Cirque du Soleil. Another important dimension to the company is that it has launched the careers of generations of young textile and fashion designers for whom it offers ideal laboratory conditions, with Leuthold acting as a peerless mentor and promoter of their talent.

With a genuine perception for the Zeitgeist instigated by a tireless search for new ideas, Jakob Schlaepfer makes a significant contribution to the definition of contemporary taste. It is therefore not surprising that the firm has been the recipient of a number of prestigious international design awards, including the Premiere Vision Imagination Prize. All Jakob Schlaepfer designs are copyrighted works created by different designers in the company's atelier.

Jakob Schlaepfer's investment in digital technology has led to the printing of designs with remarkable levels of invention and acute attention to detail.

Previous page -- This design is themed around an animal print with a difference: the digital manipulation of the pattern creates a kaleidoscopic, blurred reinterpretation of a design classic.

Above -- The creative potential of painting for digital print is conveyed in this floral motif.

Opposite page -- A print developed at Jakob Schlaepfer at a time when there was an urge to go back to analogue thinking in print design. Painting and drawing were applied and translated to digital printing in an abstract and expressive style. At this juncture the company wanted to explore a warmer language for digital print design.

Above -- A landscape motif
taken from a postcard was here
distorted and manipulated to
achieve a painterly quality.

Above -- A bold fashion print is
created by this digital montage
inspired by surrealism. The clustered
arrangement of eclectic motifs
contributes to a visual feast.

Above -- The idea for this digital print
was to create a mystic garden full of
vegetation and fruit. The result is an
intense, super-realist montage which
redefines the boundaries of the classic
floral pattern.

Marly van Lipzig

In her collection 'The Architecture of Prints', Marly van Lipzig challenges established ideas of fashion and printed textile design through an individual blend of creativity and technical knowledge.

An affinity for industrial structures led Van Lipzig to photograph the Landscape Park in Duisburg-Nord, Germany, with its dramatic abandoned ironworks and factory buildings set in regenerative landscaping. This and similar environments fuelled the aesthetic direction for this collection. For instance, photographs from the Landscape Park were used in the design 'Repetitions in Rust'.

Van Lipzig explains her design thinking in relation to the industrial photographs: 'I selected the most interesting images, those that were special because of their atmosphere, colour, composition and beautiful details. I tried to group them in different moods to distinguish them from one another, arriving at three groups.' Each group subsequently contributed to one of the designs 'Repetitions in Rust', 'Supreme Stripes' and 'Graceful Grids', each realized as engineered print designs. Colour is fundamental to Van Lipzig's aesthetic: 'The colours within the industrial architecture photographs … are a crucial element in the final print aesthetics … rusty browns, iron greys and industrial greens,' she says.

Of the relationship between prints and garment patterns in 'The Architecture of Prints', Van Lipzig explains: 'I made fifty rough garment shapes in miniature … I looked at the photographs I wanted to use and tried to match them with the rough garment shapes.' She then decided to let the shapes in the photographs define the exact outlines of each garment. 'I had to see how this would work for the 3D body, so I printed it out and traced it on to the toile fabric to check where the photographic shapes could become a pattern shape. I worked in Photoshop and at the same time in 3D.' She explains how she went on to arrive at each print design: 'I worked in a document [in Photoshop] as large as the real piece of fabric. One by one I cut out useful surfaces and elements from each photograph. After that, I arranged these elements; sometimes I duplicated them or mirrored them. I played around to look for an interesting composition.'

The fabrics are digitally printed, with the exception of screen-printed fluorescent cutting lines, which break up the industrial photographic aesthetic. The fluorescent line invites the user to cut into the print to make the garment. Each print offers two cutting lines to provide the user with a choice of two garments. Van Lipzig wanted the wearer to experience how a flat printed fabric can become a garment, and so the idea is that you buy the print, choose the garment you want to wear, cut it out, fold it and attach a few buttons where needed, and your garment is ready to wear. A sewing kit is provided with each printed fabric to support this. There are no sizes, so that almost anyone can wear the printed garment. So far, three contrasting fabrics have been used – a satin jersey, a double-sided satin and neoprene – and the choice of material has an effect on the shape of the garment. The neoprene and double-sided satin comprise two layers of satin glued to each other, and achieve excellent sculptural results. Van Lipzig imposes an important restriction on her production process: to create minimal fabric waste for reasons of both sustainability and cost.

The Japanese fashion philosophy introduced to the Western world by Issey Miyake has influenced Van Lipzig's design outlook, as she explains: 'Japanese couture has a very different approach to the construction of garments, because of the kimono. This traditional garment is flat when not worn, and hides the curves of the female body.' This made her aware of the interesting interplay between the two-dimensional and the three-dimensional, particularly a pop-up experience for a flat garment that takes its final form by being folded and put on the body. 'I love to approach the human body as an architectural space that can be manipulated, hidden or seen, depending on the message you want to get across. The Japanese have this definition of the space between the garment and the body, which possesses an important energy, called *ma*. Everything they create breathes passion and magic.'

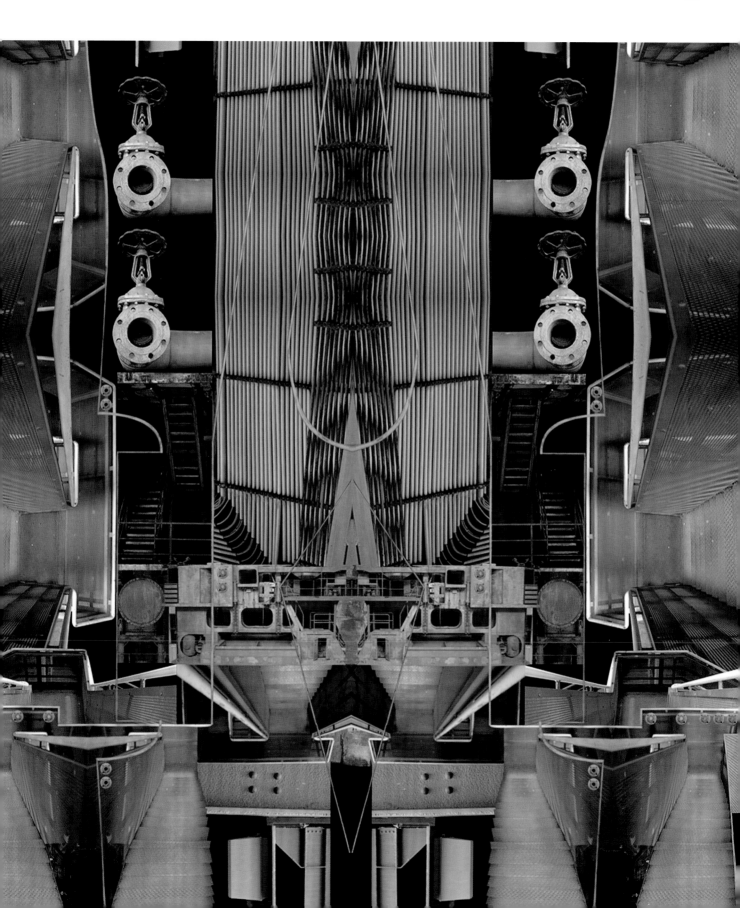

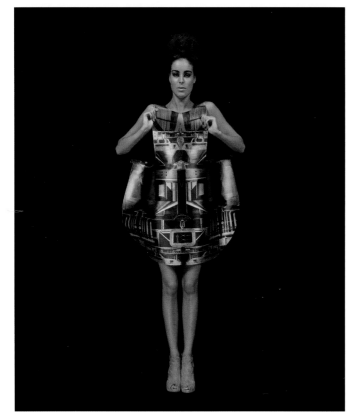
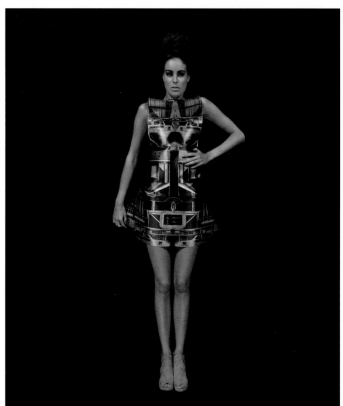

Previous page -- A digital collage of
photographic elements inspired by the
Landscape Park in Duisburg-Nord, Germany,
forms the print design 'Repetitions in
Rust'.

Opposite page -- Stages in the creation
of an apron dress from the 'Repetitions
in Rust' pattern.

Above -- Van Lipzig's design formula for
a 'Repetitions in Rust' apron dress and
tunic top.

'I love to approach the human body as an architectural space that can be manipulated, hidden or seen, depending on the message you want to get across.'

Opposite page -- This photograph, taken
at the Duisberg Landscape Park by Van
Lipzig, was the inspiration for the print
design 'Supreme Stripes'.

Above -- Stages in the creation of a
backless dress from the 'Supreme Stripes'
pattern.

Opposite page -- 'Supreme Stripes' at
FASHIONCLASH Maastricht, 2012. This piece
graphically illustrates Van Lipzig's
hyperrealistic outlook towards the
fashion print.

Right -- 'Supreme Stripes', backstage
at FASHIONCLASH Maastricht, 2012.
Photograph © Peter Stigter.

Peter Pilotto

Fellow graduates of the prestigious Royal Academy of Fine Arts, Antwerp, Peter Pilotto and Christopher De Vos are the driving force behind the fashion company Peter Pilotto. Within this partnership, Pilotto focuses on digital print and textiles and De Vos focuses on the garment forms. However, both will work beyond their realms in the pursuit of creativity. Their design approach embraces new and classical ideas of elegance inspired by notions of otherworldliness in digital print and textiles. The silhouettes and drape of their garments are inspired by sculptural shapes. Significantly, they strive to transcend established norms regarding the integration of their two fields of expertise. Each season, in what is an organic design process, Pilotto and De Vos let ideas evolve, rather than being reactionary, often bringing in ideas from preceding collections.

In 2009 Pilotto and De Vos firmly established themselves in the world of design when they received the award for best emerging talent at the London Fashion Awards. This accolade recognized their individuality, their vision and their readiness to innovate. Such qualities are evident in designs inspired by Asian subculture, such as Japanese 'light trucks' (fetishized vehicles adorned with thousands of lights), which were reinvented to become engineered digital prints in the Autumn/Winter 2012–13 collection. Equally potent in this collection were the colourful swirls of Chinese opera-mask make-up, and oversized lilac, irises and bright red carnations. This range of subjects, generated through differing drawing and painting styles, also incorporated dramatic combinations of scale, mirror-image pattern techniques and organized asymmetrical patterns, resulting in a dynamic array of aesthetic experiences with considerable impact. Importantly, the prints were imaginatively integrated into the form and movement of the garments in a graphic demonstration of the duo's boldness and originality.

While each collection develops from fresh creative impetus, there are signs of an underpinning print style that is distinctive of Peter Pilotto. When asked about their creative process, Pilotto and De Vos explain: 'Our collections are like diaries: they reflect our experiences. The Spring/Summer 2013 collection was so much about our trip to India. We find it boring to have a theme. It's always much more about a process for us. We had started working on the collection before we left, but India is so full of amazing colour combinations that of course it became part of it.' They also make the point that their brand 'is about print … but it is also about the emotional feeling you can get from colour and colour combinations'. The Spring/Summer 2013 collection was also significantly influenced by medieval and Renaissance religious art, inspired by visits to Florence and Siena. Motifs and patterns from the exhibition *Royal Manuscripts: The Genius of Illumination* at the British Library in London (2011–12) informed the prints in the 2013 Resort collection, in particular the decorative borders of sixteenth-century manuscripts.

Pilotto and De Vos give further insight into their design outlook and creative process: 'Every season our prints are about layering – it is never one simple idea. Together we create something where all the layers move to create an infinite number of patterns. We click on things as you would with a video game, and then select frozen moments to create the prints.' Themes to which they are repeatedly attracted include natural phenomena. They are fascinated by scientific views of nature, a fact that is reflected in the microscopic, encrusted, hyperreal prints in their collections. A collaboration with the art director Jonny Lu began as an exploration of generative patterns and layers, resulting in graphic, geometric prints; this approach to pattern generation is now widely recognized as an intrinsic component of their printed textiles.

The essence of the past persists in the Autumn/Winter 2013–14 collection in the interpretation of decorated works from the Spanish Renaissance, inspired by El Greco and other Spanish artists of that period. There was a sense of great novelty when the collection was shown at Tate Modern in London, with the Spanish Golden Age refracted and reimagined in digital prints. Peter Pilotto flourishes thanks to its blend of continuity and progressive thinking, and the partners' creative drive increasingly means that the brand transcends classification, a fact that is echoed in the varied nature of its audience.

Previous page -- Blue and black floral
print, Autumn/Winter 2012-13.

Above left -- Mirror-image digital print
pattern inspired by 'light trucks', the
Japanese subculture in which lorries are
adorned with thousands of lights. Autumn/
Winter 2012-13.

Above right -- Engineered print with
large-scale hand-drawn and -painted
florals, Autumn/Winter 2012-13.

'We find it boring to have a theme. It's always much more about a process for us.'

Above left and centre -- Patterns for the digital prints in the 2013 Resort collection are produced by the Print Generator, a digital kaleidoscope created specifically for Peter Pilotto by the art director Jonny Lu and his studio.

Above right -- Inspiration from Celtic and medieval patterns from sixteenth-century illuminated manuscripts is adapted into graphic, intricate, geometric motifs that define the character of the digital prints in the 2013 Resort collection.

Opposite page -- The Italian Renaissance
collides with the modern day through the
inventive use of digital technology in
this fashion print. Spring/Summer 2013.

Above left -- This engineered digital
print, inspired by trips to Florence and
Siena, captures Peter Pilotto's inventive
use of pattern, scale and composition,
and the way it can fuse dynamically with
garment and body. Spring/Summer 2013.

Above right -- The choice of pastel
colours in this collage of digital prints
echoes the tones found in Florentine
frescoes, a source of inspiration for
this collection. Spring/Summer 2013.

Opposite page -- Digital prints inspired
by the Spanish Golden Age retain a
contemporary edge through the inventive
use of collage and sculptural forms.
Autumn/Winter 2013-14.

Right -- Stained glass is inventively
translated through the powerful yet
restrained use of digital print for this
Spanish Renaissance-inspired collection.
Autumn/Winter 2013-14.

Prada

In the twenty-first century Prada has evolved to become a global brand synonymous with luxury, heritage and innovation. This success is a result of the unique outlook of directors Miuccia Prada and Patrizio Bertelli, who consistently push fashion and visual culture to new levels of creativity and quality.

Historically, Prada stood out because of the exceptional level of craftsmanship and detail in its products. This ethos continues, but with renewed vigour and focus on craft and its relationship with technology. 'Innovation involves the whole production process,' says Bertelli. 'Our way doesn't rely only on craftsmanship but also on the ability to translate that exquisite craft to an industrial level.' He outlines how the process of making products evolves: 'At Prada, each project develops through the work we put into it … We do not sit down at a table and announce: "We plan the future." It develops by degrees.'

Miuccia Prada explains the design mindset and the consequent demands: 'In fashion, once you have got something, you're already thinking about what's next. Maybe it's a little hysterical. Now every day I am thinking about change. It's a constant anxiety in general. The big deal about fashion is really very recent, this frantic pursuit of newness. It may be a good thing or a bad thing, but it's really defining this moment.'

Newness through reinvention was at the core of the Spring/Summer 2008 collection, with inspiration from sources as diverse as Liberty patterns, art nouveau, the illustrator Aubrey Beardsley and the fifteenth-century Dutch painter Hieronymus Bosch, with the Los Angeles artist James Jean fusing these elements through his twisted vision and meticulous, surrealist drawing. This aesthetic was incorporated into the design of a number of products, including printed textiles. The digitally animated film 'Trembled Blossoms' showcased the collection, including the prints, at the Prada Epicenter stores.

Print adds visual and aesthetic clarity to Prada's new concepts. In the edgy Spring/Summer 2012 womenswear collection, femininity and the motoring world collided, with materials chosen to emphasize the differences. For example, cotton was enriched with polyester in order to highlight its brightness and to make the prints more vibrant. Details such as contrasting piping and the use of leather recall the seats of luxury cars. This is a nostalgic, retro collection, with an air of optimism: sunlight and girls, 1950s hot rods and muscle cars with spiky rear fins and bodies emblazoned with flames. The iconographic language of Americana is redrawn through the lens of more than half a century of pop and style culture. The colours are sugary pastels, and pleating features, as does silk, across which race car motifs in wild patterns.

Stylistically, the prints for the Spring/Summer menswear collection of the same year are similar. Some motifs are even carried through, such as the drive-in cinema. This is a vintage range containing 1960s Palm Beach flower prints, motifs from English ties of the 1970s, and comic-book designs from the 1980s. The prints contain motifs of frenzied musicians playing saxophones, double basses and pianos, around whom an array of energetic dancers swing to the music. The odd dancer also finds her way across into the womenswear collection, moving rhythmically among hot-rod and muscle-car motifs.

The source of Prada's special design inspiration can be summarized only by Miuccia Prada: 'I like the irony in my work. It's about what I like, but also about analyzing what is and what isn't trendy, and why people like something, trying to find a way to look at it from outside, researching new ideas on beauty and femininity and the way [they are] perceived in contemporary culture.'

Previous page -- The design think-
tank AMO created this photo-collage in
Photoshop, based on a piece from Prada's
Spring/Summer 2008 womenswear collection.

Above -- The central theme of the Spring/
Summer 2008 womenswear collection
is fantasy, epitomizing the feminine
imagination. The diversity of the world
and its various interpretations is
expressed through the prints. Joyful,
almost over-the-top, they tell stories
like a comic book, with floral motifs
and original feminine figures.

Opposite page -- An AMO photo-collage
based on a piece from the Spring/
Summer 2008 menswear collection.

Above left -- Hot rods and muscle
cars race across a pastel yellow
surface. The motifs are full of energy
and a sense of speed and movement. The
confident placement and use of pattern
make for a dynamic print design. Spring/
Summer 2012 womenswear collection.

Above centre -- The classic hot-rod
flame motif is adapted into a playful
border pattern in this dress. Spring/
Summer 2012 womenswear collection.

Above right -- Cartoon and comic
illustrations capture the essence and
energy of the 1950s in the printed motifs
and pattern of this catwalk garment.
Spring/Summer 2012 womenswear collection.

Opposite page -- Detail of hot-
rod and muscle-car print design
with complementary appliquéd hot-
rod motif on a Prada handbag. Spring/
Summer 2012 womenswear collection.

**'At Prada ... we do not sit down at a
table and announce, "We plan the future".
It develops by degrees.'**

Opposite page -- The Autumn/Winter 2012-13 womenswear collection is about a contemporary woman in almost regal daytime outfits. The concept revolves around fantasy, such as that of a cartoon or video game, with prints a key element. Geometric, abstract and Jacquard prints are shown in orange, purple, white and military green. Graphic prints combine with plastic embroidery and Swarovski stones.

Right -- The prints in the Spring/Summer 2011 womenswear collection are a reinterpretation of the Baroque and feature such motifs as bananas, monkeys, pineapples and cherubs. They alternate and are mixed with many different kinds of striped print. They are always exaggerated, even in the combinations of bright colours, from orange and light blue to shocking pink with a South American attitude.

Vivienne Westwood

English design rebel Vivienne Westwood is internationally recognized as a global fashion icon. She has built this reputation on strongly held beliefs, original design thinking and dedication, qualities she has drawn on over the decades to produce phenomenal fashion collections. While it is true that Westwood does not follow any fashion rule book, the quality of her collections shows considerable technical ability in the making of her garments and accessories, a fundamental factor in enabling her to convey her unique ideas. Her studio has adopted an admirable attitude of leading not following, a way of thinking which has persisted throughout Westwood's career. From the culturally revolutionary 'Punk' style of the 1970s to her recent collaboration with the Ethical Fashion Initiative, Westwood's work demonstrates her willingness to take risks and make strong social, cultural and political statements through the medium of design. In the book *Vivienne Westwood*, curated by Terry Jones of *i-D* magazine, she explains: 'I do have reasons for what I do. I am a very political person, and I really think if you put these clothes on you will look like a force to be reckoned with.'

The Ethical Fashion Initiative is a project run by the International Trade Centre, a joint body of the United Nations and the World Trade Organization. It aims to empower, support and provide an income for women in Africa and the developing world by creating work and access to an international market for artisans and micro-producers. In doing so, it seeks to reduce dependency on aid – the slogan 'Not Charity, Just Work' has become synonymous with the project. Vivienne Westwood has collaborated for many years with the Ethical Fashion Initiative on a range of printed and beaded bags, handmade in Nairobi, Kenya.

Westwood's work for the Ethical Fashion Initiative shares certain characteristics with her iconic 'Punk' style. In both, a bricolage of talismanic motifs is used for sartorial display, and improvisation and resourcefulness are on display. These qualities echo African craft practice, in which, for example, necklaces are fashioned from unlikely items such as old car hubcaps. The Vivienne Westwood Ethical Fashion Initiative bags are made from reused and discarded materials – canvas, roadside advertising banners, leather off-cuts, and brass melted down in the slums of Nairobi from gathered pieces of discarded metal. Importantly, the quality of the final products has met the demands of Westwood's design aesthetic.

Print features throughout Westwood's fashion collections and has been a key factor in defining her as a fashion icon. The prints used on the Ethical Fashion Initiative bags are inspired by African fabrics, and in some cases are informed by fashion prints from previous Westwood collections, such as the squiggle print from her swashbuckling 1981 'Pirate' collection.

To mark the 2012 Olympic Games, held in London, Westwood designed the collections that became known as 'Britain Must Go Pagan'; an ethically produced bag for the menswear market combines in its print English and ancient Greek iconography. The word 'Sex' is emblazoned on the surface of another bag, a direct reference to the name of Westwood's first boutique on the Kings Road in London. Also printed on the bag are the words 'Craft must have clothes but truth loves to go naked'.

In essence, Westwood is interested in building an intellectual framework for her designs through a critical evaluation of her working methods, which draw on references from history, culture and politics. She interprets and transforms these into innovative fashion statements.

The prints used on the Ethical Fashion Initiative bags are inspired by African fabrics, and in some cases are informed by fashion prints from previous Westwood collections.

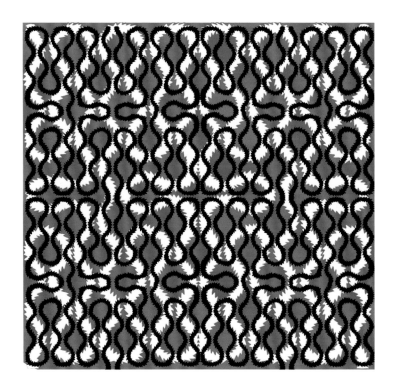

Previous page -- The 'Greek Eye' design, which has been realized as a printed holdall made from recycled materials as part of Westwood's involvement in the Ethical Fashion Initiative.

Above and opposite page -- Inspiration for the Spring/Summer 2014 'Squiggle' design came from Westwood's Autumn/ Winter 1981-2 'Pirate' collection. Through a number of reapplications of the iconic design, this pattern is set to become a design classic.

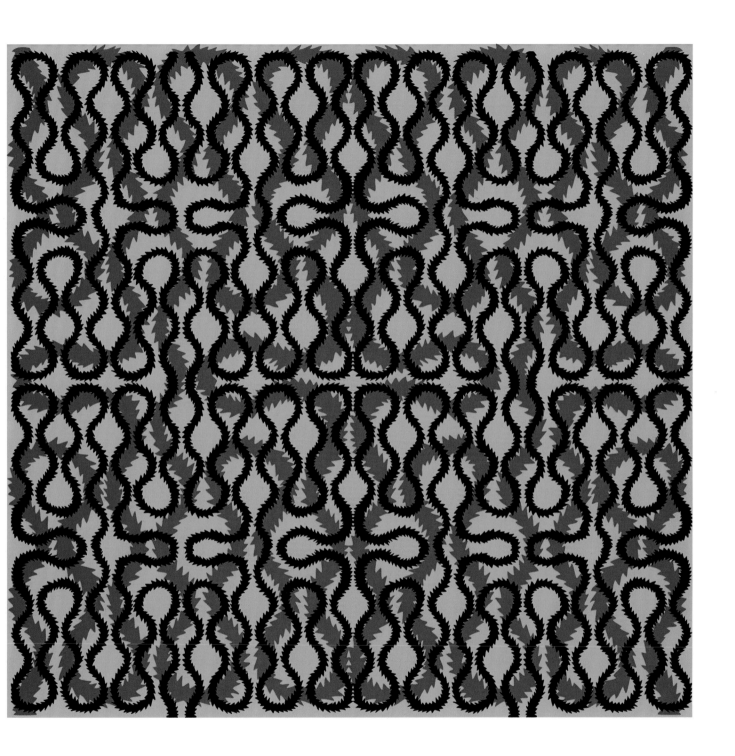

Opposite page -- 'Green Tiger' print, with
rucksack and holdall, designed for the
Ethical Fashion Initiative.

Above, clockwise from top left -- 'Sex'
and 'Get a Life' shopper bags, made for the
Ethical Fashion Initative, 'Greek Relay'
holdall and 'Climate Revolution' shopper.

'I do have reasons for what I do.
I am a very political person ...'

Above -- 'War and Peace' holdalls,
designed for the Ethical Fashion
Initiative.

Opposite page -- 'War and Peace' design.

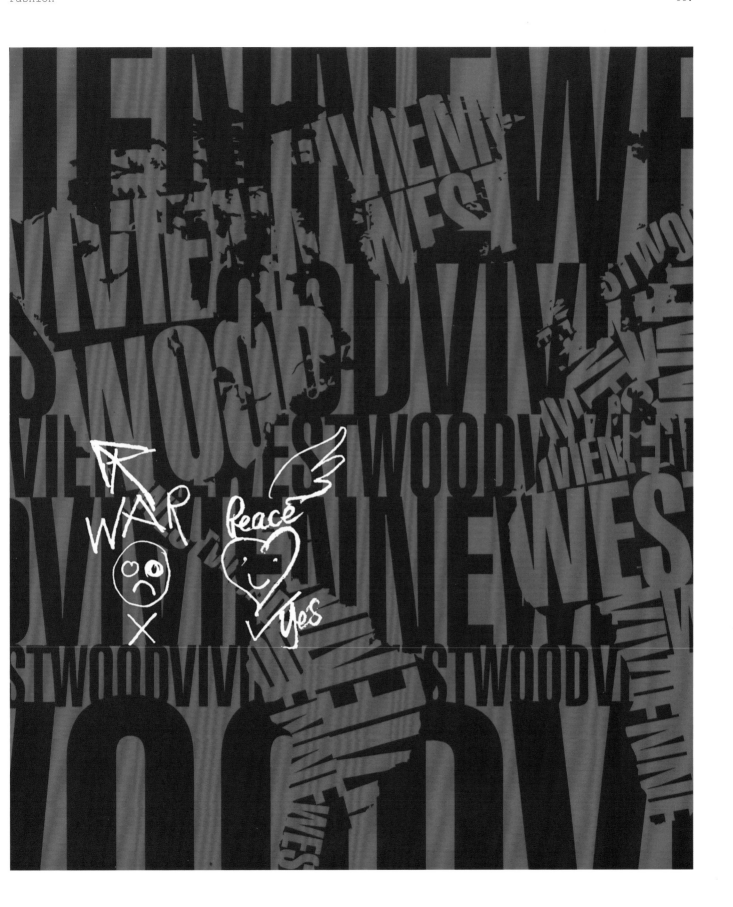

Interiors

Interior spaces and their surfaces and furnishings present significant opportunities for experimentation in print. With this in mind, this section examines new thinking within a medley of concepts, processes and aesthetics. The eclectic selection chosen here showcases original designers, studios and collaborations from around the world, innovators who challenge established perceptions of print within the interior setting. As the vehicles through which ideas are presented, technology and substrates are of course explored, and print designs are illustrated as standalone images, on products and within interior settings.

Collaborations between textile manufacturers and artists are not a new phenomenon, but the interaction between the two creative disciplines is currently generating a rich pool of original designs. This approach has been adopted at the legendary Scandinavian company Marimekko, which collaborated with painter Astrid Sylwan to capture the essence of her abstract painting on furnishing fabrics. ROLLOUT is another inventive studio producing a broad mix of conceptually driven wallpapers. The designs are created in-house or are the result of collaborations with like-minded artists and designers. They respond in a creative way to unique commissions: for the Woods Hole Inn near Martha's Vineyard, for instance, the wallpaper was inspired by the discovery at the inn of two boxes of room check-in cards, dating from 1946. The innovative Maharam Digital Projects employs a different strategy again, including printing to order. This new thinking has begun to provide greater choice for the consumer and is liberating interior spaces from traditional conventions.

Among small batch producers of interior textiles there is evidence of innovation and originality. One example is Deborah Bowness, who takes photographs of furniture, clothing and other everyday items and transforms them into *trompe-l'œil* wallpapers which then end up in a variety of interior, display and site-specific contexts. New design histories are being created in the design of wallpaper and interior prints, whether by Marimekko or Bowness. These ambitious and bold practices are a result of new thinking in design and they are now transforming and redefining the parameters of the field of interior prints. This is principally because designers and textile manufacturers have been prepared to take a chance on new ideas and the discerning customer seems to appreciate this mindset.

Whether in a domestic or corporate setting, the prints have an effect, both sociologically and psychologically, on the physical space and its occupants. This is a quite different encounter from the fluid fashion print. Intelligent print design is now providing new experiences for the home, office and other forms of built environments. The appearance of the household and the corporate sphere is changing in the twenty-first century through reformulation of traditions, with the new design tools of the digital age often facilitating the depiction of new subjects.

Anna Glover

The London-based designer Anna Glover has an original outlook. She has a flair for using drawing, painting and computer-aided design to generate individual ideas, which she transforms into designs with charmingly surreal, bizarre tendencies.

An ever-evolving approach to research plays an important part in Glover's design process, as she explains: 'I have built up a huge collection of books, postcards, magazine clippings and printouts, all of which really excite and inspire me.' Glover finds London an inspirational place, and – despite having lived there all her life – continues to be excited by it. She says: 'If ever I am stuck for ideas, one of my favourite museums or galleries never fails to help get things moving again.'

Glover, who had a lot of experience in designing fashion prints, wanted to test out ideas for interiors on a small scale at first, and came upon the idea of using a doll's house made by her father. At first she used the empty house as a three-dimensional mood board, collecting ideas and images and putting them on the walls and floors. Her clear idea of the mood she wanted to create in each room had a real impact on her choice of colours. In the bathroom she wanted to create something rich and exotic: the 'Jungle' design. She says: 'I imagined it to look good in the daylight but also by candlelight. When I thought about all these things combined, luscious greens and gold came to mind.' She wanted the children's room in the doll's house not to be gender-specific, and so she created the wallpaper 'Space Dinosaurs', which is intended to appeal to both boys and girls. Glover says: 'In my opinion, there is often too much of a divide where interior products are concerned. Some girls like space rockets and dinosaurs too! When I first created this design, it was definitely leaning

more towards a boyish print, so I chose to insert the pink and the mint green, which I think lifted the design a little and gave it a more feminine touch.'

Drawing is at the core of Glover's design ethos; colour and composition, although equally important, always follow. She explains: 'Once I have decided what will go into a design, I draw or paint the elements separately in the chosen style and technique. For example, the space dinosaurs were drawn with a fine black liner and then scanned and coloured in Adobe Photoshop. This method of working allows a lot of flexibility as far as texture and colour are concerned.' However, this is not a set method of working; in the 'Jungle' design the plants were painted in gouache, then scanned and set up to repeat on the computer. On seeing the full repeat, Glover found the design far too heavy for the bathroom, so she broke up the repeat to allow more space and light into the room.

The 'Space Dinosaurs' design shows Glover's bizarre, playful imagination. She outlines the concept for the design: 'I guess I like to create a story even if it's just one that entertains me while I'm working on it. This particular design is about a world where dinosaurs work in a rocket launch pad powered by energy created through biomass gasification. They gather the plants and flowers and put them into a machine that burns them, and in turn the energy released from this process is transformed into electricity that powers the rocket launch into space. "Space Dinosaurs" is simply a pattern made up of key motifs from the story.'

'Lobster Garden' is a design Glover is working on for a room divider screen as part of a collaborative project with two other artists, who are focusing

on the construction of the screen and the application of her design to its surface. The initial sketch illustrates the fact that the lobster garden forms only a section of the whole design. Glover explains: 'The idea behind this is that this landscape depicts the world inhabited by all the other designs in this collection. The luscious garden is filled with unusual plants and overlooks the more industrial valley where the biomass gasification factory sits. The dinosaurs are the guardians of the land, and they tend to the gardens and manage the factory. They are also partial to lobster thermidor, so they keep lobsters in the lake for special occasions. … I am totally obsessed with the idea of knocking people out of everyday reality, even if just for a moment. As kids we got to do this every time we heard a bedtime story, and I like the idea of trying to recreate that.'

'If ever I am stuck for ideas, one of my favourite museums or galleries never fails to help get things moving again.'

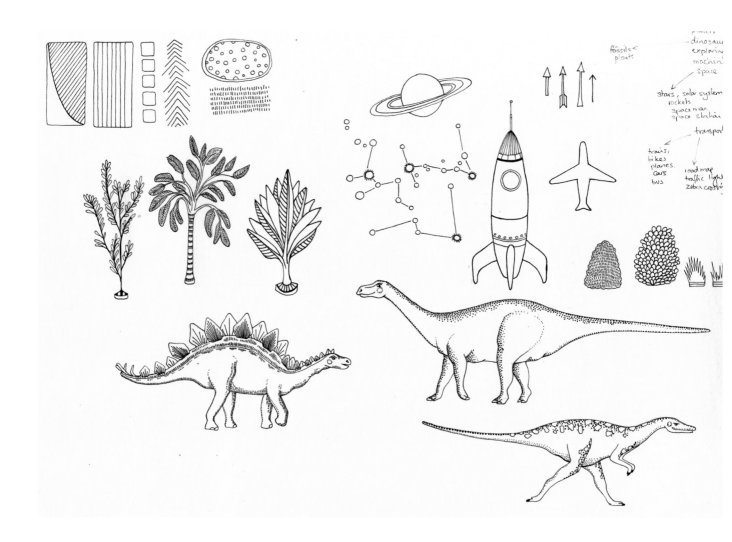

Previous page -- The 'Monkey Kingdom'
design, part of the surreal interiors
collection, is a beautiful yet
unexpected jungle garden. The monkey
kingdom to the west of the vast gardens
is where the monkeys prefer to spend
their time. 'This is chiefly to do with
the abundance of the naturally occurring
boiled egg, which is a delicacy among
the monkeys,' explains Glover.

Above -- Preparatory drawings of
dinosaurs, plants, planets, rockets
and other motifs for 'Space Dinosaurs'.

Opposite page -- 'Space Dinosaurs'
embodies the inventive spirit that
underpins Glover's creative philosophy.

Opposite page -- 'Lobster Garden'.

Above -- Preparatory sketch and painting for 'Lobster Garden'.

'I like to create a story even if it's just one that entertains me while I'm working on it.'

Above -- 'Jungle' installed in the bathroom of Glover's doll's house.

Opposite page -- 'Jungle' shows off Glover's craft as both an illustrator and a print designer.

Astrid Sylwan for Marimekko

Belgian-born Astrid Sylwan, who is based in Stockholm, is one of Sweden's leading abstract painters. Her large works explore the materiality of paint and the presence of colour. Sylwan outlines her approach: 'It is just as important how the paint is applied as what actual colour pigment is used. The same blue can have many different characters and expressions depending on how it is applied to the canvas. It can be painted, poured, dripped, sponged on, etc. Painting is a physical activity. The brush-strokes mimic the rhythm of the body and become a visual trace of the force or gentleness with which [the paint] is applied.' Sylwan seldom uses traditional fine-art tools, instead preferring to work with carefully selected do-it-yourself or industrial painting tools.

The paintings capture light and space, time and place, and draw on Sylwan's state of mind, which can oscillate between control and improvisation. She explains: 'I work on a painting until it starts to respond, talk back and find a balance, its own universe. There needs to be a structure, a compositional skeleton to hold the painting together, but not too rigid, so that it can vibrate. Somewhere on the brink of collapse is where I want to stop, where the painting cannot be deciphered in one look but forces the eye to wander and discover.' This process is direct and intuitive and reflects the way Sylwan sees and experiences things such as art, music, weather, scenery and conversation, which connect with her emotions, including love, anger, confusion and curiosity.

While Sylwan is distinctive in her practice, she acknowledges such influences as the Dutch painter Per Kirkeby and, in print, the quality and craftsmanship of Josef Frank and William Morris. Sylwan is an advocate of handcraft rather than digital methods, as she feels that in the digital aesthetic certain qualities can be lost.

The collaboration between Sylwan and Marimekko developed from a phonecall from Minna Kemell-Kutvonen, the company's chief designer. Sylwan instantly hoped that this was an approach for her to work with the company, and that is exactly what followed. She summarizes the challenges the project created: 'At that time, none of us could grasp how much work it would take … I had to be taught the basics of everything, as I had no textile print education or experience.' The project required close collaboration with Petri Juslin, manager of the artwork studio, and because of the complexity of the painted pattern it developed into a project that pushed the boundaries of print knowledge at Marimekko. The commitment required to pull the project together demanded that Sylwan make numerous trips to Helsinki: 'In retrospect, I am glad I didn't know the hours, days and weeks the project would consume. I will definitely work with Marimekko again, but we agreed to wait a few years so we all feel hungry for it again.'

The design, called 'Vattenblänk' ('shimmering water'), resembles a contemporary painting. Its gradient effects, overlapping colours and scale of repeat arguably place it in the domain of art rather than of industrially produced products. However, Sylwan is clear that 'Vattenblänk' and her other designs for Marimekko, 'Irrbloss' and 'Samum', are not reproduced paintings: 'Although my initial reaction when I got the offer of doing a collection for Marimekko was positive, I did give it a lot of thought. There is a clear distinction between an original work of art and a mass-produced object. If I had taken a finished painting and transferred it on to products, it would have been problematic. I could think of nothing worse than the classic abuse of fine art that you can encounter in any museum shop around the world.' That said, Sylwan was clear that the designs needed to retain the qualities of her painting, and display a similar energy: 'That is why we have kept so much of the drips and smudges. Cleaning it up would kill it a bit. At the same time, I want it to be stunningly beautiful. We started with trying to merge my ideas with the possibilities and limitations of printing.'

In 'Vattenblänk', the emphasis is on movement, whereas in 'Irrbloss' ('will-o'-the-wisp') inspiration comes from the fantastical creatures that flutter over swamps, now embedded in the mythology of various Western cultures. Sylwan's third design for Marimekko, 'Samum', is an art fabric, sold by the piece. In it she attempted, in her words, 'to catch a warmth and light spiced with a slight desperation and a little sadness. "Samum" is the name of a desert wind, a demanding wind – one that claims to make people unravel, in a similar way to the mistral wind of southern France. It is romantic, adventurous, beautiful and demanding, like a good story, and full of warmth and light. The vibrant reds, oranges and yellows suggest desert heat and glare, while the overlapping globular shapes impart texture and depth, evoking the inverse of the dry desert wind – rhythmically dripping teardrops of water.'

Previous page -- Sylwan feels that the
print 'Samum', which has no repeats, is
therefore closest to her paintings.

Above -- Sylwan at work in her studio
in 2011.

Opposite page -- 'On the Far-Away Horizon
of Consciousness', painting, 2011.

'Painting is a physical activity. The brush-
strokes mimic the rhythm of the body
and become a visual trace of the force or
gentleness with which [the paint] is applied.'

Opposite page -- 'Vattenblänk', flat fabric length showing repeat. Movement is the essence of this repeating print. It is like water in a stream: blue, with deep shadows and yellow highlights that catch the eye.

Above left -- 'Vattenblänk' plate, bowl and cushion.

Above right -- 'Irrbloss' bed-linen. *Irrbloss* ('will-o'-the-wisp') is a phenomenon of eerie lights that occurs in swamps when marsh gas ignites. There is a long history of myths attached to these lights, as they were thought in the old days to be fairies and ghosts. It is a beautiful, sudden and unexpected light.

Deborah Bowness

Deborah Bowness creates unique *trompe-l'œil* wallpaper using photographic and photomontage styles, challenging the traditional perception of wallpaper to the extent that her pieces could be described as functional works of art. Depending on the nature of the collection or project, the subject may vary; for example, Bowness has worked from photographs of her own vintage furniture and clothing to great effect.

Reinterpreting the world with photography and a hand-painted colour palette, Bowness produces collections that are simultaneously playful and sophisticated. She is a risk-taker who will explore and try out new ideas, rather than being content to follow trends. Bowness explains her creative approach: 'My work is a continuum. The objects I photograph and turn into designs stand together as a whole collection. It is as though I am furnishing and decorating a space that exists only in my head. The frocks hanging on the walls explore the notion of decorating with objects out of context … looking at everyday objects and then making you look again. I try to re-present everyday objects to make the viewer appreciate beauty in the banal.' In relation to her use of photography, she explains: 'I generally take all my own photographs using black-and-white film. But sometimes when I am working to commission I will be given images to work with.'

Most of Bowness's wallpapers are hand-printed in small batches, using pre-exposed silk screens. There are exceptions: wallpapers made to order often use hand-cut stencils rather than pre-exposed screens, and feature more printed colours and hand-painted detail. There are also digital prints, which provide an opportunity to include a wider range of colours in a single design.

In addition to wallpaper, Bowness has designed paper-based items such as her 'Cut Outs', life-size objects printed on billboard paper. On her design process and its flexibility, Bowness says: 'I am always open to whatever is happening when I am supposed to be working on something. I don't believe you can truly control creativity … it's something I channel and observe.' She is happy for an idea to evolve over time, and believes a piece of work will land in her collection when it lands: 'I have many ideas I have been working on for years, and when they are ready they get presented in the collection.' However, when working to commission she acknowledges that there must be deadlines. The process can be straightforward or challenging, she says, 'depending on the energy or time constraints. Sometimes I make the straightforward challenging.' She works with a range of design tools, both analogue and digital, and is happy to mix them, but she does admit that lately she has been spending time on the computer and has, on occasion, found it difficult to pull herself away.

Bowness's choice of colour contributes significantly to the style and atmosphere of her work, particularly when it is *in situ*. She explains her approach to colour: 'I don't think about colour, I see it. And it either looks right or it doesn't. All I have to go on is my instinct. I use black-and-white photography, so the original colours are not recorded, except maybe in my memory. I make decisions about how I will colour it when I am looking at it … But then as I print wallpapers I have the pleasure and opportunity of seeing objects in different colourways, and trying out things that you would not normally see. Hand-painting colours allows me to add the human touch; I like the loose marks made by the watercolours I use.' If she is aiming for a true representation of a photographed object, she will use full-colour digital printing, a method she has now begun to explore and work with more frequently.

Bowness has worked on a number of commissions, the earliest of which was for Sotheby's on an outdoors theme. For that, she drew on an image from a camping holiday in Portugal. In another commission she designed wallpaper for display in the windows of Selfridges, for which – despite being given a brief – she was left to develop her own themes. She chose to juxtapose the central London location of Selfridges with images of more 'real' places, those she considered to have more soul. Bowness also spent a year working with Polydor Records on a variety of installations for different departments in the company. She explains: 'Each department had their own idea of what they wanted to be photographed and turned into wallpaper. Once themes were agreed, we worked together to find locations … I got to go to a few gigs and an amazing analogue recording studio.'

'Paper Trail', an outdoor exhibition of wallpaper and cut-outs, takes Bowness's work into the urban street environment of Brighton. Some works are discreet, while others are bolder, pasted up around the city on walls that have inspired her. These works challenge the viewer to explore the process of domestic displacement, creating stage-sets and still lifes in unexpected locations.

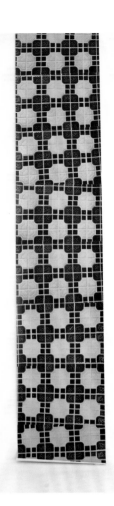

'I try to re-present everyday objects to make the viewer appreciate beauty in the banal.'

Previous page -- Designs from the
'Utility Lamps' wallpaper range.

Opposite page -- 'Blue Kitchen Cupboard'
from a special edition of cut-out
furniture paste-ups, printed by machine
and coloured using hand screen-printing
and paper stencils on billboard paper.

Above left -- 'Utility Brown Cupboard',
from the special edition of cut-out
furniture paste-ups.

Above centre and right -- 'Tile D'
and 'Tile E' from the 'Utility Tiles'
wallpaper collection.

Opposite page -- Folding decorative
screen with mixed panels from the
wallpaper collection, featuring
designs from the 'Wallpaper Frocks'
and 'Utility Chairs' ranges.

Above -- Drum wallpaper, designed for
the Polydor Records commission.

Right -- Selfridges window display:
'I liked the idea of juxtaposing
the swish central town location of
Selfridges with images of places more
real and with soul,' says Bowness.

**'It is as though I am furnishing and decorating
a space that exists only in my head.'**

Opposite page -- 'New Antique Books'
from the 'Bookshelves' wallpaper
collection on display in Bowness's
'Paper Trail' art project.

Above -- Floral domino pattern
from Bowness's 'Paper Trail'
art project. Dominos is an old
method of creating wallpaper on
sheets, rather than on rolls.

Dorte Agergaard

Danish designer Dorte Agergaard established her eponymous design company in Copenhagen in 2008. In a relatively short period of time, Agergaard has become recognized internationally for her individual approach towards design, which has led to her work being selected in recent years to appear in exhibitions in New York, Paris, London, Milan, Cologne and Shanghai.

Agergaard first studied graphic design at Central Saint Martins College of Art and Design in London, followed by textile design at Kolding School of Design. This creative background, coupled with a conceptually motivated vision and a passion for photography, has defined both her core values as a designer and her aesthetics. Her approach takes visual form in digitally printed textiles which convey her photography in varying manifestations. Agergaard's decision to work in the medium of photography is a result of a random experience – in her words 'an experiment combined with a mistake' – driven by a curiosity to see if it could be possible to take printed textiles into a whole other world.

The subjects of Agergaard's photographs come from nature and from everyday objects found in interior settings. The photographs, which are often enhanced using Photoshop, are then digitally printed, with the resulting fabric applied to products including pillowcases, curtains, Venetian blinds, duvet covers and wall panels. When Agergaard works with landscape motifs for interiors, nature is represented in a hyperrealistic way, in part a consequence of the digital enhancement of the original photograph. This hyperrealistic vision intentionally brings the outside into the interior setting and aims to challenge our perceptions of how we look at our surroundings. It also generates an atmosphere that possesses

more than a hint of the surreal and echoes of *trompe l'œil*.

Agergaard is keen to point out that she does not conform to traditions, to the extent that her work does not draw on the rich heritage of repeat pattern in textiles. The reasons behind this attitude are simply to help her achieve the right conditions in which to create her unique designs, which are more akin in many ways to engineered print designs for fashion. While she avoids repeat patterns, Agergaard does explore pattern in refreshing conceptual ways, particularly in the two interesting projects '7 Views' and '7 Days'.

In '7 Views' she created a collection of photographic digital prints in collaboration with the interior textiles company Kvadrat, which were exhibited in Milan. The project involved the photographic documentation of views from the windows of her apartment, as Agergaard explains: 'The pictures were recorded over three to four weeks, where every day I took pictures of my view at around 2 pm and 3 pm.' The photographs were taken during the spring because of the unique qualities of light and colour specific to this season. By choosing these views she consciously wanted to bring a personal element into the documentary process and subsequent printed outcomes.

In the '7 Days' series, the concept and process are interlinked to tell a story from everyday life: a documentary study of Agergaard's unmade bed in the morning over a period of seven days. The results are seven different sets of digitally printed bed-linen, each named after a day of the week.

Inspiration for the 'Pure Nature' and 'Pure Home' collections came from Agergaard's photographs of nature and everyday objects. In the 'Pure Home' digital prints

she celebrates the beauty of 'ordinary' things that surround us in everyday life: shoes, tables, plants and floorboards. But in a strange way they seem to transcend their status and become almost larger than life and super-real because of their clarity and sharpness.

Agergaard believes that constant change is the only reliable factor in this life. This view is mirrored in some ways when she considers her inspiration: 'I renew myself and find inspiration by observing … I can easily sit in an "empty terminal" and get ideas.' She continues: 'Everyday reality gives me substance … I do not follow sensations or trends.' Having lived most of her life in Denmark's cosmopolitan capital, a recent move to the countryside resulted in a focused period of photographing nature, drawing on untamed aspects of nature and other realistic motifs from the coastlines of Denmark and Sweden during midsummer.

Previous page -- Blind from the 'Interior
Dialogues' collection, shown at 100%
Futures in London.

Above left -- Digitally printed duvet
cover from the '7 Days' collection.

Above right -- Photographic digital
print from the 'Pure Home' collection.
A photograph of Agergaard's old apartment
relocates one reality into another.
The idea, 'was to use our "normal"
surroundings as patterns, and to see
the contrast in printing a very physical
space on a textile.'

Opposite page -- The 'Pure Home'
collection is intended to highlight and
celebrate the beauty of 'ordinary' things
which surround us in everyday life:
shoes, tables, plants, floorboards.

Agergaard intentionally brings the outside into the interior setting and aims to challenge our perceptions of how we look at our surroundings.

**'Everyday reality gives me substance …
I do not follow sensations or trends.'**

Opposite page, left to right -- 'Water
and Sky' and 'Landscape', manipulated
photographs digitally printed on to
cotton, from the collection 'A Piece
of Fabric'.

Above, left to right -- 'Heaven', 'A Leaf'
and 'A Flower', manipulated photographs
digitally printed on to cotton, from the
collection 'A Piece of Fabric'.

Eugène van Veldhoven

The Dutch textile designer Eugène van Veldhoven is known for his erudite capabilities in the application of traditional and contemporary manufacturing technology to create progressive textiles. Because of his ability to generate innovative aesthetics in his textiles through a fusion of design and varied manufacturing techniques, he has established a formidable client base in the world of textiles, including Jakob Schlaepfer and Maharam.

For his portfolio, Van Veldhoven uses a suitcase which contains pieces made using between 20 and 25 techniques, some innovative and others quite simple. He regularly updates this portfolio, motivated by a number of factors, as he explains: 'There is an inner drive to keep improving my portfolio … I have to prove to myself time and again that I can still do it. There is an ambition to surprise my customers – there's some vanity there … And I want to sell.'

Van Veldhoven's creative process begins with the selection of a technique or theme, followed by weeks of designing patterns on the computer and finding fabrics to go with them. After these development stages, the application of the patterns or treatments to the fabric can take a matter of hours. Van Veldhoven may use 'high-tech' methods, but always in a simple, direct way. Significant is his ability to visualize results at the point of designing at the computer.

Van Veldhoven is disciplined with his use of time, and manages the demands of his profession, such as organizing travel to see clients, attending trade fairs and visiting mills, even though that means he can go for weeks without drawing a single line. Then, however, as he explains, 'I make a break, disconnect the telephone and email and draw, draw, draw.'

Almost all his design samples are ready for production, and he can advise on the sourcing of chemicals and places where the sample can be produced in larger volumes in western Europe. Some of the more experimental samples can create challenges in that two or three different machines or factories may be needed. In these circumstances, he explains, 'you have to find clients who can afford a higher cost price, be lucky to find a factory or a region that happens to combine these techniques, or adapt your design. And preferably in that order.'

The Textile Museum in the Netherlands invests in state-of-the-art machinery, and Van Veldhoven works with this machinery and its technicians a few times each year, as well as getting involved in projects at the museum. When the museum purchased its first inkjet printer and then its first laser machine, he was commissioned to challenge the museum's technicians to push the technology to its maximum potential. He also regularly works at the Stork factory in Boxmeer, where machinery is built for the manufacture and treatment of textiles, including coating, printing and hot-melt techniques. He also talks to chemical suppliers: 'When I find a new technique, I arrange to work at the machine at least once, either at a mill or at the company that builds the machinery. It's important that I understand how the technique works.' He also emphasizes the importance of being able to understand the vocabulary associated with a manufacturing process so that he can explain it to clients.

In recent years, Van Veldhoven has given increased attention to the pattern in a design. On this subject, he says: 'With every new series, I challenge myself aesthetically. At the moment, for instance, I am designing a series of inkjet-printed patterns where I use photographic images of flowers. I want to show the beauty and richness in colour and texture of flowers, which obviously are clichés in textiles. So I also want them to be modern; suited for modern interiors … And it is starting to work.'

Van Veldhoven is in no way a stylist, waking up in the morning and saying: 'Today the colour is red.' Rather, he says, 'I think about a lot of things (my friends say I think too much). I feel like I have to work hard; why am I making this? What's the point, who will use it?' He also makes the important point that samples 'can be a bit of an intellectual challenge, or a game I play with myself. I need more than just "beauty" to judge my work by the end of the day.'

'I feel like I have to work hard; why am I making this? What's the point, who will use it? ... I need more than just "beauty" to judge my work by the end of the day.'

Previous page -- This floral print combines digital inkjet and burn-out printing. It was showcased at the prestigious Trend Forum at the trade fair Heimtextil, Frankfurt, in 2013.

Opposite page -- Here the designer worked on to an already flocked fabric surface. The flocking process involved screen printing using adhesive ink. Flock fibres are then sprayed over the wet print. The flock is made static while being sprayed, so the fibres all land upright in the glue, giving a rich velvety look. The viscose fibres are tiny - between 0.5 and 1mm long. After printing and flocking, the fabric is cured at 140°C.

Above left -- Horizontal strips of foil are applied to a felted substrate in this experimental design.

Above right -- Industrial orange/ yellow polyester lace printed all over with glass beads. The beads are perfectly round, about 1mm in diameter, and colourless, so they work as small magnifying glasses. The magnification is particularly obvious in this detail, where it stresses the different colours of the weave. Here the glue was coloured red, and the fabric is a woollen tweed.

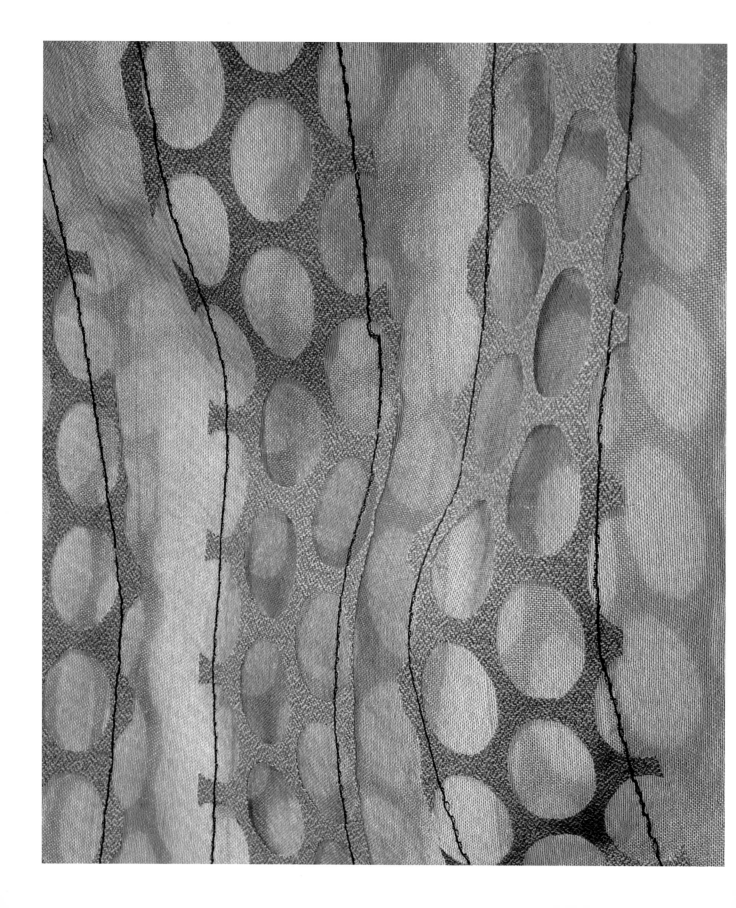

Opposite page -- This 'devoré' print
(from the French 'to devour') involves
the printing of a paste containing sodium
hydrogen sulphate on to blended fabrics
containing cellulosic fibres (cotton,
viscose) in combination with either
protein fibres (silks) or synthetic fibres
(rayon, polyester). Through a process of
heating, chemicals in the paste eat away
at the cellulosic fibres to reveal the
semi-transparent remaining fibres.

Right -- Irregularly pleated polyamide
tulle with heat-sublimation print. The
heat from the sublimation printing sets
the pleats, but as the fabric is an open
weave it remains loose and flexible.

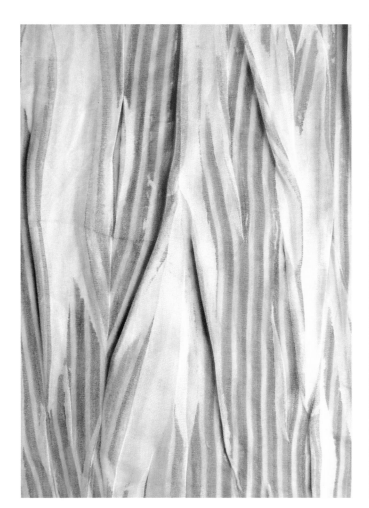

Above left -- Striped design on pleated
polyester, made by dye-sublimation
printing, a process which uses heat to
transfer dye on to fabric.

Above right -- This fabric results from
pleating followed by digital inkjet
printing. Van Veldhoven explains: 'I
tried to design a pattern that is
only possible to achieve with digital
printing; the repeat height is around
2 metres, and I let every colour slowly
fade into another. That's a subtlety
that's very hard to get with screen
print or rotary print.' He continues:
'I used stripes because it's nice
to have a strong graphic element to
combine with the irregularity of the
pleats.' Van Veldhoven used a digital
printer with a short conveyor belt
to enable the fabric to be fed into
the print as flat as possible.

Opposite page -- The innovative
'Scales' fabric is a combination of
dye-sublimation printing and laser-cut
fabric, which is then embroidered on to
a backing cloth of the same material.

Iris Maschek

After graduating from the University of Applied Sciences in Krefeld, Germany, Iris Maschek established her own design company in Cologne. Building on her design education and early business experiences, she has gone on to work with a range of international clients in the textile and interiors markets, including interior textiles company Création Baumann. Her innovative design achievement was recognized in the product design category of the prestigious Red Dot Awards in 2010, for her progressive wallpaper 'Park'.

In addition to supplying an array of international clients, Maschek creates her own line of unique printed wallpapers, affording her the freedom to explore darker, more experimental imagery, which could be described as Modern Baroque, while simultaneously minimalist in style. This digitally generated aesthetic gives her wallpapers an illusory depth. When displayed in their intended interior settings, the wallpapers take on the characteristics of over-dimensional paintings, with an infinite delicacy rendered by her perceptive use of line work.

Maschek regards her work as a never-ending, lifelong process, and her design concepts express this philosophy. Free thinking is an early stage that naturally leads to the formation of her concepts. The concept itself is a fundamental step for Maschek, providing the structure in which to compress certain aspects of her free-thinking, intuitive ideas and imaginings. The practical starting-point for the development of her work can vary, she says: 'Sometimes the origin is a simple drawing I made, sometimes it is photography of organic structures: crystals, plants, liquids, stones. I'm fascinated by pictures made by a scanning microscope or fractals. The starting material then undergoes a process of several analogue and digital workings.'

Maschek uses a limited colour palette – predominantly black and white – as a statement of minimalism, simplicity, strength and purity. The objective, she says, 'is to call the spectator's attention to what the design's essence is in itself, and not to distract them from that.'

The designs 'Ava' and 'Krom' give a more specific insight into Maschek's ideas. 'Ava' is a good example of her obsession with layering lines and structures to create highly complex designs. 'Working on "Ava" took me a long time and was like a deep dive into an ocean of fragments, reduced floral shapes, graphic elements and drawing traces,' she says. '"Ava" is also my attempt to exhaust the possibilities of digital printing with an eye on magnitude and dimensioning of a wallpaper design.'

Maschek sees the wallpaper 'Krom' as a simple, reduced piece of work in comparison to 'Ava': 'My idea was to create an abstract pattern that works as a small repeat. Images I had in mind working on this were historical echoing, traces you leave on ice when skating on it, and the surface of an old table that shows tracks of everyday use. I also like the idea of human existence leaving traces on blank paper.'

Maschek likes to assign names to her wallpapers to evoke ideas and fantasies in the beholder and to support the character of the design. She says: 'By giving the wallpapers titles or names, you bring them to life for real. You could say that for me my designs don't exist until I have given them a name.'

When designing new wallpapers, Maschek is acutely aware of time frames and deadlines, and the simple fact that they can't be ignored, but she is keen to say: 'Nevertheless, I always pay close attention to my intuition and rely on my feelings whether a design is finished or not.' She makes the point that she will not be rushed to put her work out unless she feels absolutely sure it is finished to her specific design standards: 'It's always my aspiration to provide perfection in my designs. I can feel it when a design is ready to see the light of day.' Once a design is completed, it is sent to a digital wallpaper printing company for manufacture. Apart from checking samples and colour management when relevant, Maschek leaves production of the wallpaper in the hands of the printer, which prints it on demand.

Maschek enjoys getting involved in art projects, such as one connected with the Russian avant-gardist El Lissitzky. She says that she likes to walk the line between art and design; Lissitzky similarly crossed that line, influencing the European avant-garde of the 1920s.

Previous page -- 'Krom' (detail). While
working on the graphic elements of this
paper, Maschek was thinking of ice-
skating and the tracks the skates leave
behind. The name 'Krom' is intended to
represent the sound made by the skates
scraping and rasping over the ice.

Above and opposite page -- With 'Ava',
Maschek's aim was to create a wallpaper
with a dark, strong, twisted and highly
dramatic character. As she was working
on it, she saw an early film noir by
Robert Siodmak, *The Killers* (1946). This
atmospheric film, characterized by stark
lighting and deep shadows, stars Ava
Gardner, who gave the wallpaper its name.

'It's always my aspiration to provide perfection in my designs. I can feel it when a design is ready to see the light of day.'

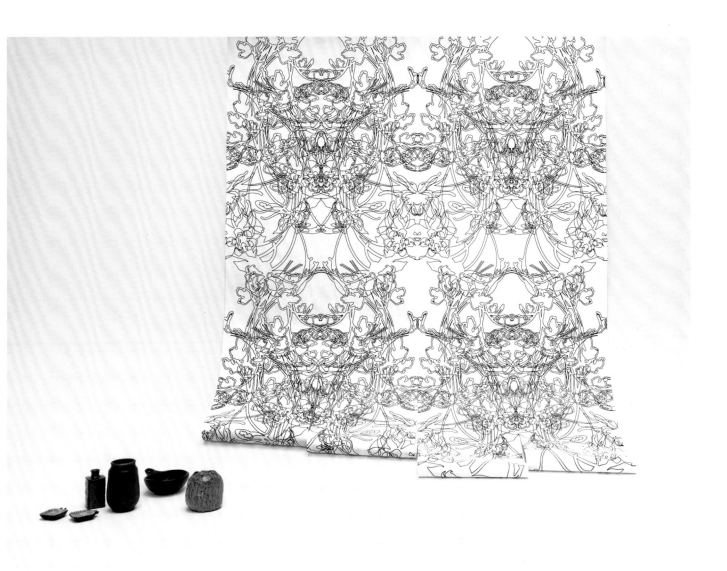

Opposite page -- The digitally designed
and printed wall panel 'Shade' illustrates
Maschek's creative prowess in working with
line. The result is a delicate, rhythmic,
three-dimensional pattern.

Above -- 'Lun Chrome' reflects Maschek's
ongoing interest in large-scale digital
design, which follows a core creative
formula involving inspirational thinking
and intuition.

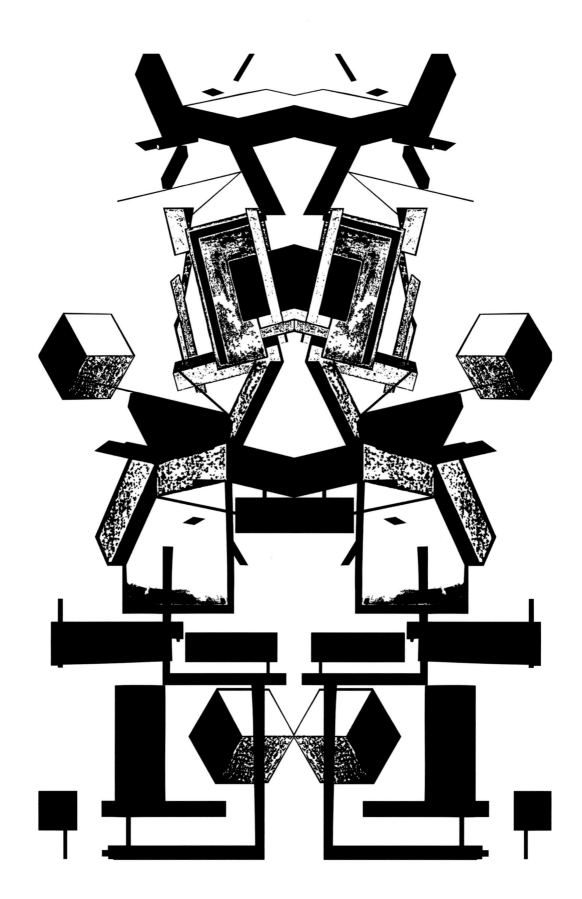

Opposite page -- The 'Lissitzky' paper
is an example of Maschek's involvement
in art projects. In this case she
examines and re-interprets the work of
the Russian avant-gardist El Lissitzky.

Above -- 'Arc Chrome' reflects
Maschek's desire to experiment,
generating a contemporary alternative
to a traditional chandelier.

Maharam Digital Projects

Maharam Digital Projects is a collection of digitally printed wall installations created by emerging and established artists, photographers, illustrators and fashion and graphic designers. Maharam, which provides textiles for commercial architects and interior designers, realized that, although digital printing had evolved substantially, it was under-used in interior settings. The project evolved both from this awareness that the market had failed to couple cutting-edge technology with sophisticated content, and from the fortuitous discovery of Wallpaper LAB. Run by Ron Keyson, Wallpaper LAB produced digital art installations by a select group of artists and was looking to expand. Maharam seized this opportunity, realizing that its strength as a company, its relationships with long-standing collaborators and its previous forays into the art world would allow it to have curatorial influence. From this fusion, Maharam Digital Projects was conceived as an interdisciplinary forum that exists at the convergence of art and design.

A curatorial committee decides whom to collaborate with, and potential partners are evaluated on such criteria as their reputation, the appropriateness of their work and how well it could translate into digitally printed wall art. It is fundamentally about how much the committee and Michael Maharam, the principal of Maharam, like the work.

A team first visits the studio of the contributor, who is then invited to Maharam's headquarters in New York. Usually, the contributor has an idea they want to work on, although occasionally Maharam influences his or her direction. Conversations vary in each case regarding the selection of artwork and how it is translated into a wall installation, since every artist works in a different way and has their own creative idiosyncrasies. For example, for Cecilia Edefalk's work 'Coastal Plants', all 200 of her paintings had to be scanned and digitally arranged. Markus Linnenbrink's large multimedia painting 'Stolenmoments/FirstofMay/Brasov/Romania1969' required other considerations, resulting in the decision to photograph this large work in sections, which were then stitched back together digitally in preparation for printing.

Once the artwork has been identified, the process of preparation and conversion into a wall installation is usually straightforward. The work is digitally photographed, scanned into the computer, adjusted where necessary and then prepared in an appropriate file format for digital printing on to the vinyl substrate using water-based printing inks. Getting such details as colour correct can take time, and the contributor remains involved in the process, receiving a strike-off for approval. The time frame from first collaboration with an artist or designer to final production can vary from two months to two years.

The Dutch artist Karel Martens has created a number of wall installations for Maharam. He was part of the '1 of 10' pattern initiative of 2009, when Maharam invited ten graphic designers to produce ten patterns each, with the idea that the 100 resulting designs would provide insight into the modern language of pattern, its common elements and distinguishing characteristics. 'Dutch Clouds' by Martens came out of this project. While it is not completely clear how Martens created the pattern, Maharam knows that he used a 'secret recipe' of thousands of highly complex multicoloured icons to recreate a photograph of the sky taken the day his grandson was born.

The iconic Swiss furniture company Vitra has a close relationship with Maharam. In 2010 Michael Maharam visited Switzerland to present the Maharam Digital Projects to Vitra, whose campus architect at the time, Till Weber, selected projects to install in the flagship VitraHaus in Weil am Rhein, designed by Herzog & de Meuron. These included the piece 'Taurus' by artist Sarah Morris. The installations were directly applied to the wall, and Weber selected furnishings from Vitra's collection to create complete environments. The installations formed part of the Art Basel show in 2011.

Finding a balance between pleasing the contributors aesthetically and making the product durable to meet clients' expectations is a challenge for Maharam. All wall installations are produced to order and are customizable. Pieces may be scalable according to parameters for minimum and maximum size established by each contributor, repeatable (can be multiplied out in seamless succession without affecting scale) or configurable (comprising tiles that can be rearranged).

Previous page -- The print 'Ye Olde Ruin'
by the Turner Prize nominee Paul Noble is
a segment from a larger piece of the same
name. Noble's elaborate work is based on
fictitious city and town architecture.

Above -- 'Renard 2' showcases the creative
mind of the designer Harmen Liemburg. In
this digital collage of archival woodblock engravings he generates a new story
that is both playful and mischievous.

Right -- 'Renard 1' (detail). Here
Liemburg assigns new roles and meanings
to individual images, resulting in a
surreal narrative.

Opposite page, top -- 'Dutch Clouds' by
Karel Martens reflects the designer's
fascination with optical illusions and
surprise, as well as his belief that it is
important to play with ideas of reality.

Opposite page, bottom -- Markus
Linnenbrink's photo-drip work
'Stolenmoments/FirstofMay/Brasov/
Romania1969' (2010) has been ingeniously
translated on to vinyl and conveys both
narrative and abstract qualities.

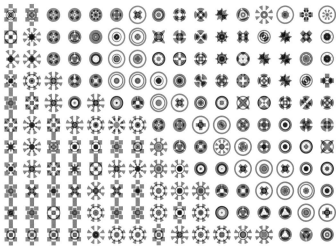

Above -- 2x4's collaboration with Maharam
resulted in 'Tableau Vivant', a study in
controlled chaos, conveying a dense landscape
of gods, mythic beasts and mortals.

Above and right -- In 'Coastal
Plants', Cecilia Edefalk conveys her
interest in seriality. This simple yet
dynamic composition is formed of 200
watercolours of the European coastline,
painted over a three-year period.

Opposite page -- Sarah Morris originally
created 'Taurus' in gloss house paint.
As a digital textile print, it remains
both highly dimensional and super-flat,
with bright shapes in a grid. Morris's
irregular patterns are inspired by the
urban architectural environment.

Maharam Digital Projects was conceived as an interdisciplinary forum that exists at the convergence of art and design.

ROLLOUT

Toronto-based creative studio ROLLOUT designs and digitally prints wallpapers under the direction of Anita Modha and Jonathan Nodrick. Over a relatively short period of time, ROLLOUT has created unique wallpapers that sit well within the context of the twenty-first century. Inspiration comes from photography, graphic and industrial design, as well as from other fields. To meet self-imposed creative demands, the company collaborates with innovative artists and designers while at the same time producing experimental in-house designs, a formula which has attracted clients from all over the world.

The birth of ROLLOUT came about thanks to Nodrick's acquisition of an under-used large format printer, which came with strings attached: Nodrick had to build a business around the printer if he was to acquire it. His first initiative was an art show called 'Rollout', an exhibition of art wallpapers created by his friends. The brief was to create what they thought wallpaper could be. As a consequence of the exhibition Nodrick realized there was an opportunity to push the boundaries of interior textiles. From these early beginnings a fundamental philosophy has evolved: to provide more innovation, more creativity, more art and more individuality.

'Worth' is one of a number of remarkable wallpapers designed by Nodrick and is a collaborative piece with Modha. The design fuses punk rock, granny and brothel themes to achieve a beautiful yet eerie comment on voyeurism and vanity. Nodrick explains: '… from a distance, the decorative filigree draws the viewer into the gaze of a wall filled with x-rayed human skulls. These "mirror mirrors" reflect the impending decay that will one day wither our beauty and strip away our youth once and for all. Its ominous call challenges us to live, work and party hard.'

The 'Wayfinder' wallpapers present the viewer with quite different conceptual and visual experiences. The graphic symbols are both decorative and functional, generating new possibilities for architects, interior designers and space planners. The duo behind the designs are Maaike Evers and Mike Simonian, who first met ROLLOUT in New York in 2007, but it was not until 2010, when they had an idea that really excited them, did they discuss a collaborative project. The end results were the 'Wayfinder' wallpapers. Evers and Simonian provide a snapshot into their working methods: 'We like moving from brain to hands and back and forth. This might involve some reflection time at our secret spot overlooking the San Francisco Bay, some hot glue gun experiments, working with real materials in the workshop, 2D and 3D explorations on the computer and finally lots of constructive disagreements to distil ideas down to a point where we are both excited about them.'

A collaboration with American artist David Palmer resulted in a collection of wallpaper designs titled 'Oh, That Explains Everything'. The designs explore the open-ended dialogue of where value lies; chalk-board drawings portray past, current and future theories of value and the conversation that flows between them. Numbers, formulas and diagrams are freely combined with pictograms originating from various disciplines such as economics, science and sports as well as less rigorous systems like games of tic-tac-toe and hieroglyphic counting systems. Palmer keeps journals that date back to his freshman year of college, explaining: 'they are a combination of sketchbook, diary, scrapbook and idea repository, and I always have one with me. There is a numbered encyclopedia set of them on a shelf in my studio. They are the primary tools I use for getting stuff out

of my brain and on to paper.' He continues: 'The challenge for an artist is to create work that's of our time, that's relevant to our increasingly complex world, but that also embodies a strong personal vision.'

While renovating the property, the owners of the Woods Hole Inn, near the Martha's Vineyard ferry station, discovered two boxes of room check-in cards dating from 1946. Water-damaged and torn, the cards meticulously documented names, dates and room pricing for each guest. The owners of the inn contacted ROLLOUT to create a custom design based on the room cards. Scans of the cards are assembled in a repeat pattern, with the weathered patina of time a deliberate feature in the aesthetic of the wallpaper. Recently debuted at the opening of five new rooms on the second floor of the inn, the design is a living testament to times spent on sandy beaches, family bonding and the pleasures of relaxation.

Finally, when Nodrick was questioned on important ideals and beliefs to follow as a creative company, he explains: 'I think it's having confidence in being creative, possessing the skills to execute new ideas in new ways, as well as having a sense of natural curiosity. These qualities are in the people or organizations I want to collaborate with, regardless of the specific market they operate in.' This mindset has so far served the company well with a string of innovative wallpaper solutions and progressive projects.

'The challenge for an artist is to create work that's of our time, that's relevant to our increasingly complex world, but that also embodies a strong personal vision.'

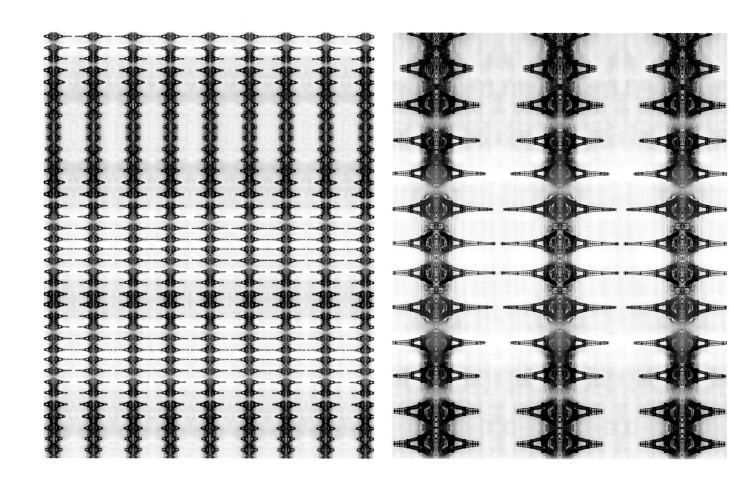

Previous page -- 'Worth' wallpaper, designed for the Artist series.

Above left -- 'Construction Eiffel Tower' from the 'Wanderlust Paris' wallpaper collection. This series portrays landmarks, transit, contemporary photography and classic works by French artists such as Degas and Monet in a drive to inspire the concept of travel.

Above right -- 'Construction Eiffel Tower' (detail). The design came about after Nodrick found a collection of photos that were taken from the same spot for every month in which the tower was being constructed.

Opposite page -- 'Le Corbusier' wallpaper (detail), by photographer Petra Reimann for the Artist series. While browsing on Facebook, Nodrick saw a photograph taken by Reimann of a building designed by Le Corbusier in Berlin, which caught his interest. Nodrick explains: 'There was something about the colours in contrast to the concrete and using the architecture and perspective to create a sense of depth that I wanted to try out as a wallpaper.' Reimann in Berlin approved the use of her photograph and the wallpaper was born.

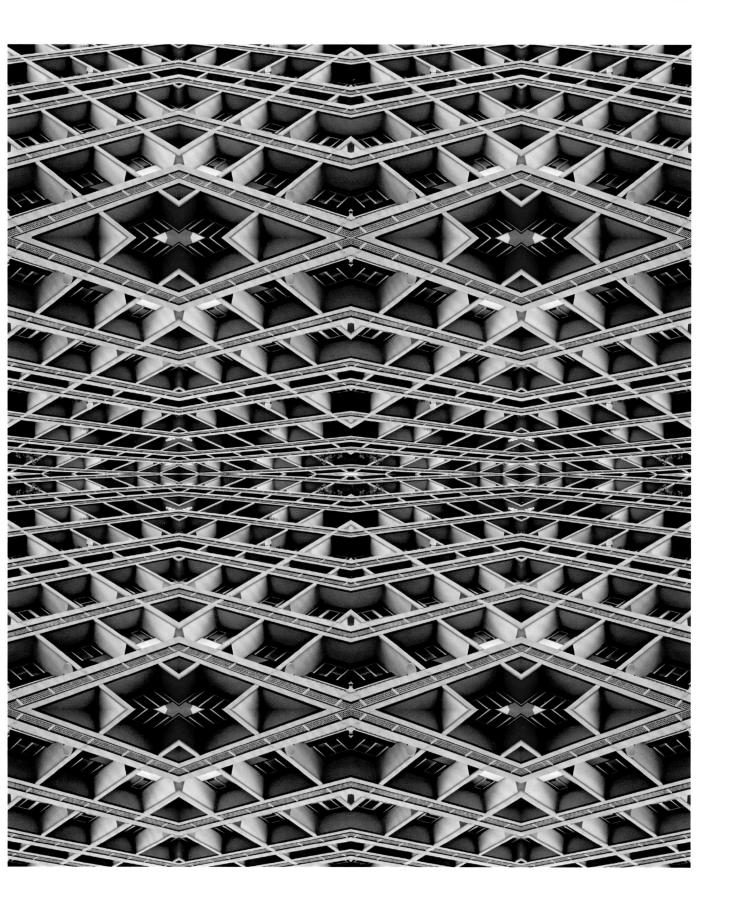

Above -- 'Stripes' wallpaper design for
Holt Renfrew. Holt Renfrew is revered as
Canada's largest luxury fashion retailer.
'Stripes' is a seasonal backdrop for
their window displays.

Opposite page -- 'Sultry Hair', wallpaper
repeat pattern by illustrator Andrio
Abero for the Artist series. This pattern
is now incorporated into many different
types of spaces, including the Marquee
Nighclub and Dayclub at the Cosmopolitan
Hotel, Las Vegas.

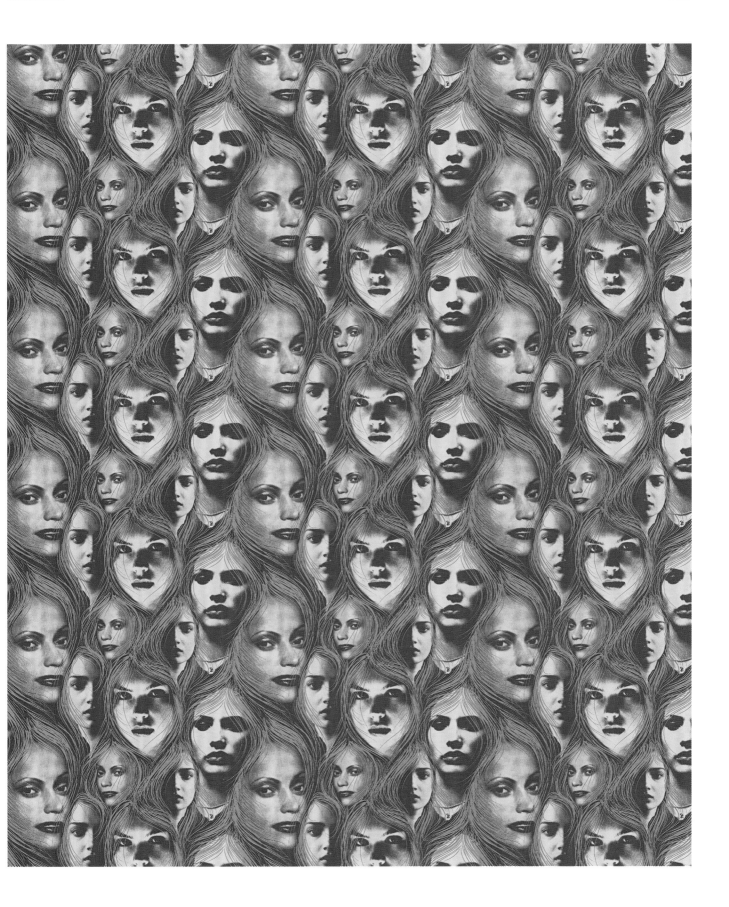

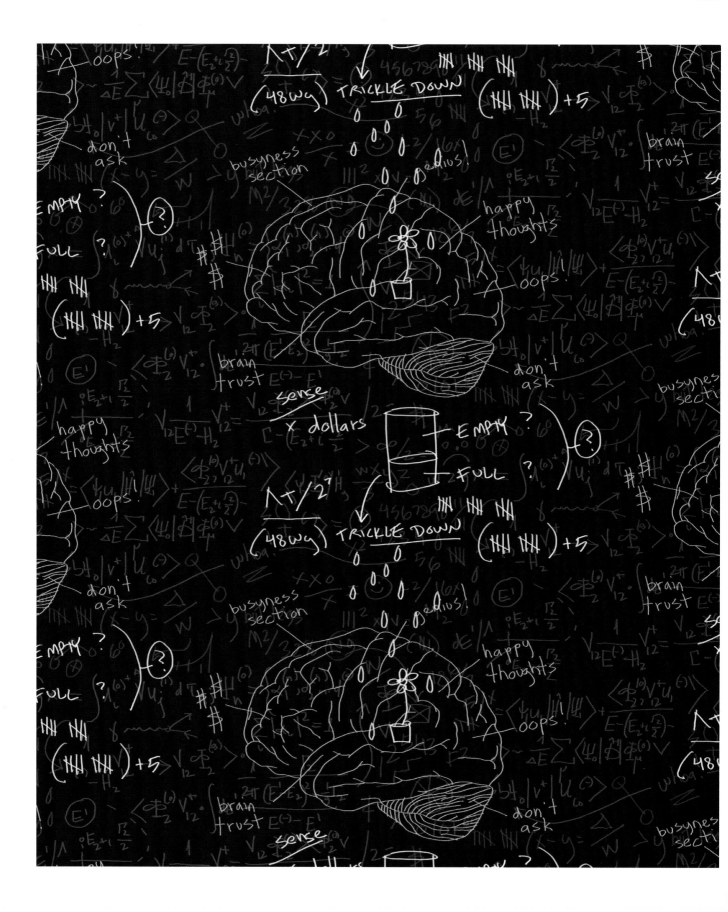

Opposite page -- 'Trickle Down' wallpaper, from a collection of designs titled 'Oh, That Explains Everything' by David Palmer for the Artist series.

Top -- Custom wallpaper installation for the Woods Hole Inn, Martha's Vineyard.

Right -- 'Wayfinder Arrows' wallpaper installation by Maaike Evers and Mike Simonian for the Artist series.

Timorous Beasties

The remarkable company Timorous Beasties, whose name is taken from a poem by Robert Burns, is a collaboration between Alistair McAuley and Paul Simmons, who joined forces a few years after graduating from Glasgow School of Art. They have created an iconic brand specializing in design-driven interior fabrics, wallpapers and related products.

They started out in a slightly unusual way, as Simmons explains: 'We really felt there was a market for a lot of the designs we were producing, but we couldn't find anyone to take us on, and the only solution we could come up with was to produce our own work ourselves.' This decision gave them creative autonomy, as he continues: 'We can design and produce whatever we want, we can spend even a couple of years working on something.' Their design ethos is therefore different from that of the mainstream, because they do not have to answer to anyone.

The brand's emphasis is on quality combined with provocative and experimental design. This mindset was cemented in the iconic 'Glasgow Toile', a contemporary interpretation of the classic French toile de Jouy. 'Glasgow Toile' depicts the darker side of urban social realism against a backdrop of familiar Glasgow landmarks, significant to McAuley and Simmons because of their proximity to where the pair lived and worked for a number of years. The atmosphere generated in this design is sinister yet funny, and a moral intent underlies the visual narrative. For example, a junkie shoots up in a notorious graveyard called the Necropolis, where drug addicts go. The moral is that if you shoot up, you will literally end up in a graveyard. Other landmarks include the Charles Rennie Mackintosh Church in Maryhill, an area where McAuley and Simmons had a studio. The design of 'Glasgow Toile' created

technical difficulties: in order to be organized into a toile format, elements of the original drawings had to be overlapped as well as gaps added to create a greater range of tonal qualities. In order to create continuity between aspects of the scenes, they had to be joined together with horizontal lines. 'Glasgow Toile' has been successfully followed by London and New York versions.

All design work is done at the brand's Glasgow studio, where they continue to hand-print many of their fabrics and wallpapers. McAuley and Simmons are aware that there is a generic look in what they do; for example, they tend to work on a large scale and use many different methods of production from the hand-printed to the digital. An important part of their design process is that they design for production. Simmons explains: 'You have got to think about how [the design] is going to be produced. What we try to do is mix some of the technologies together; you might have a digital print, then we might well bring that print back into the studio and hand-print on top of it.'

While their work is contemporary, it is rooted in tradition, as demonstrated by their reinterpretation of the toile. They are passionate about certain traditional qualities, such as academic drawing and complicated repeats. When they have been extremely experimental and taken risks, it has worked in their favour indirectly, making them money and bringing other gains in terms of credibility and publicity.

Simmons provides intriguing insight into their design ideology: 'I like to think that we design things people were not expecting to like, and I think when you ask someone what they do like in terms of textiles, music, books or anything like that, the only reference they

have is something they already know. … What we try to do is to give something to people that they never realized they wanted.'

McAuley and Simmons draw inspiration from numerous creative sources, including the textile designers Josef Frank and William Morris, the artists Joseph Beuys, Paul Klee and Pablo Picasso, the films of Ridley Scott and such objects as Italian motorcycles.

Timorous Beasties' fabrics can be relatively costly. This is because production methods are labour-intensive for certain designs. The profit on these types of designs can also be quite small.

Previous page -- 'Glasgow Toile' reflects
characteristics of a classic toile but
with a difference: the narrative conveys
the darker side of contemporary society
in Glasgow.

Above, left to right -- 'New York
Toile', fabric and wallpaper. This toile
captures street life in Manhattan, in a
similar vein to the 'Glasgow Toile'. The
versatility of its elements can be seen
in its configuration as both fabric and
wallpaper.

Opposite page -- The creative 'Fresco'
wallpaper is an inventive combination of
a distressed floral fresco background with
overprinted pearlescent coloured dots.

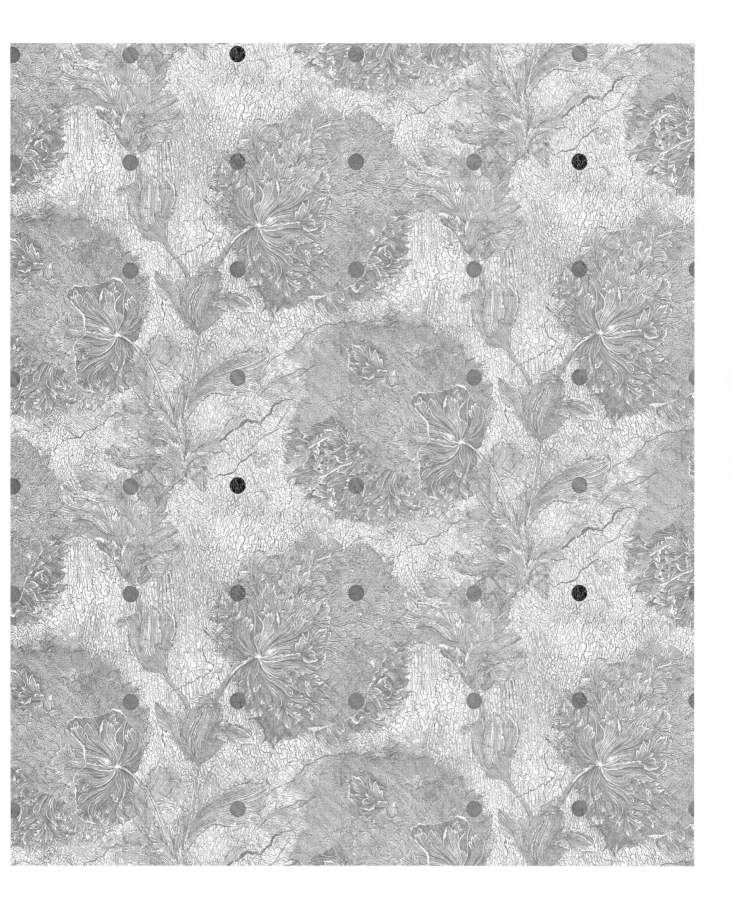

'What we try to do is to give something
to people that they never realized
they wanted.'

Opposite page -- 'Cloud Toile' wallpaper
provides a sense of the ethereal and
transcendental through the stylized motifs
of cloud formations.

Right -- 'Hunting Toile' wallpaper
illustrates traditional country life
through sporting pastimes of shooting
and fishing.

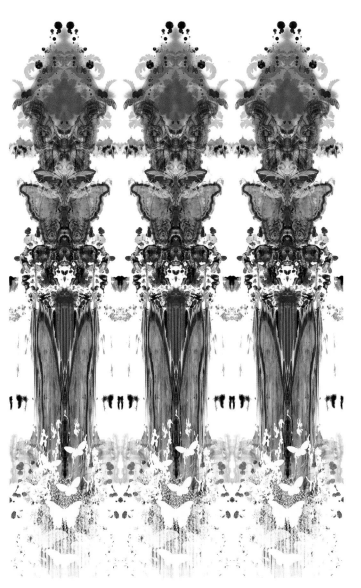

Opposite page -- At a glance 'Devil
Damask' wallpaper appears to be a
classic decorative design, but on closer
inspection it is possible to discern more
than a trace of the 'devil' within the
repeating pattern.

Above left -- The experimental 'Butterfly
Totem Damask' wallpaper is realized
through digital and hand-printing
manufacturing methods.

Above right -- 'Omni Splatt' fabric
inventively works with mirror-image
pattern generation in this expressive new
design direction for Timorous Beasties.

Todo Muta

Laura Molina and Sergio Herrera are the visionaries behind the creative studio Todo Muta in Seville. With combined expertise in fine art and design, they tackle an eclectic range of fashion and interiors projects within a broader portfolio. The name of the studio is a reference to their innovative philosophy; Spanish for 'everything mutates', it represents what Molina and Herrera do in their creative practice. They aim to give products a new 'skin' that will convey a message.

Exploring new products as a conduit for their concepts and iconography is central to the studio's philosophy. The challenges this presents require Molina and Herrera to be on a continuous learning curve, gathering knowledge and skills in unfamiliar methods of production.

While Todo Muta draws on similar creative principles and processes to those used by others in the visual arts, Molina describes the studio as 'a team operating as a creative machine'. This creative machine expands or contracts depending on the project and the expertise required. In this process the fusion of art and design is a key recurring ideological concern.

When involved in a commission, Molina and Herrera discuss with the client the product that is to be developed. They then move through the phases of the creative process: research, documentation and analysis; initial sketches; digital treatment of drawings; prototypes; and the final presentation of the product. This methodology is similarly applied to personal projects, but with other considerations, as Molina explains: 'We start by reflecting on what we want to design, the main theme, what the collection will include or what type of production we are going to apply, cost analysis, distribution channels, etc. Finally, we work on the product's presentation campaign and the relationship with the media.' She acknowledges that they have greater freedom with personal projects: 'There's normally a common thread … You can sense this from the subjects we choose … This common thread is what gives meaning to our work.'

A unique project for Todo Muta was commissioned by an architect and hotel owner for the Hotel Rural. Molina explains: 'From the very beginning we thought the project was very interesting as it required the design of various graphic ranges and their application to different objects: rugs, chairs, walls, dinner services, etc.' They had to draw inspiration from the hotel's location, the Andalusian landscape of olive trees deep in the olive oil-producing region of southern Spain. Details from the location, such as tree bark, the fur of local animals and objects used to harvest olives or store oil were used to inform their drawings and designs.

Inspiration for the 'Warriors' collection evolved from the representation of different heads that reminded them of animals, shamans and magical characters. Gradually, they realized that the heads could become an army, and the idea of 'Warriors' was born. Without losing sight of the initial idea, they developed the heads to enable them to be applied to contexts such as T-shirt prints and snowboard surface patterns. 'Jaw' is another intriguing project, orientated around the jaw-bone of an animal, transformed into printed cloth and applied to fashion and interiors.

Drawing is one of Todo Muta's core creative tools. All initial sketches produced by hand are subsequently explored in the digital domain, and such aesthetic concerns as colour, composition and pattern are investigated. Once the artwork is finalized, production files are prepared according to the substrate and product form. Molina explains: 'One of the things we really love about our work is the mixture between something handmade using "traditional" methods, and new technology for treating and printing images.'

The customers and clients for Todo Muta's unique work are those who are interested in things outside of the norm, as Molina explains: 'We're aware that we move in an area of certain ambiguity where we don't fall in with the traditional art circuits or work within the demands of the market.' What they have begun to observe is that traditional retail and media channels for art are beginning to take notice of cross-disciplinary studios like Todo Muta, as they can see opportunities for product innovation.

Social issues are of interest to Todo Muta, which aspires to combine traditional production processes from other parts of the world with its iconography to generate new products. In the future, Molina explains, their aim is 'to work directly with communities with certain work process know-how. These would be projects in which the importance would lie not only in the final product but also with all that surrounds the working process. We want to recover, preserve and give value to these processes. At the same time, we would widen the scope of our vision, sharpen our wits and bring in renewed energy to Todo Muta.'

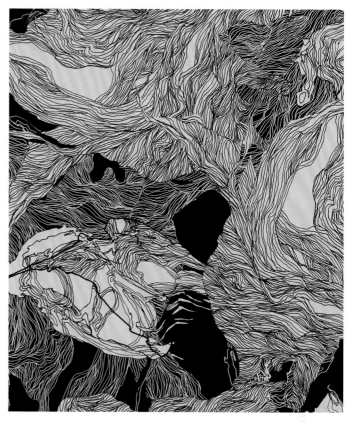

'One of the things we really love about our work is the mixture between something handmade using "traditional" methods, and new technology for treating and printing images.'

Previous page -- The formal layout of
this design, dictated by the motifs
of traditional oil containers, is
distinctive in style and conveys
historical and cultural associations
with rural Seville.

Opposite page, clockwise from top left --
The irregular oval motifs are suggestive
of the olive, evoking the atmosphere
of the agricultural geography of the
land around Jaén in southern Spain. --
This abstract pattern is an inspired
interpretation of olive bark, a trace
of the local Spanish environment. --
Finished printed textile samples for the
'Hotel Rural' project. -- A multicoloured
print from the 'Hotel Rural' project
with a variety of elements including a
transparent overlay of animal-pelt motifs.

Above left -- This printed textile
design from the 'Herborea' collection
is inspired by artificial environments.
Molina and Herrera play intelligently
with ideas of technology and nature,
an artificial nature, created by models
in three dimensions based on natural
structures.

Above right -- From the 'Herborea'
collection, this rhythmic pattern creates
dynamic visual space through the way in
which line and colour are combined.

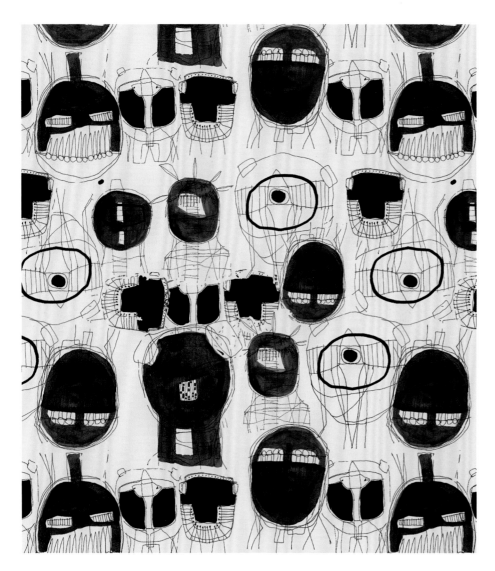

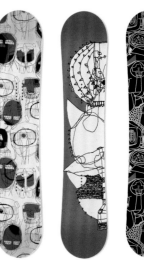

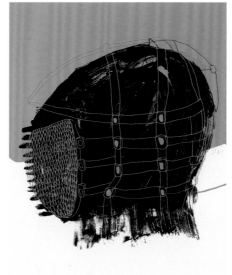

Above left -- This design from the 'Warrior' collection shows Molina and Herrera's experimental outlook conceptually and through the medium of drawing. This collection has evolved from the representation of different heads, including those of animals, shamans and magical characters.

Above right -- Without losing the original design ideas, finished designs are applied to various items, including snowboards.

Bottom -- Single painted motif of a head from the 'Warrior' collection.

Opposite page -- This design is inspired by basket-weaving. As a surface pattern it has multiple potential applications, including fashion and interiors.

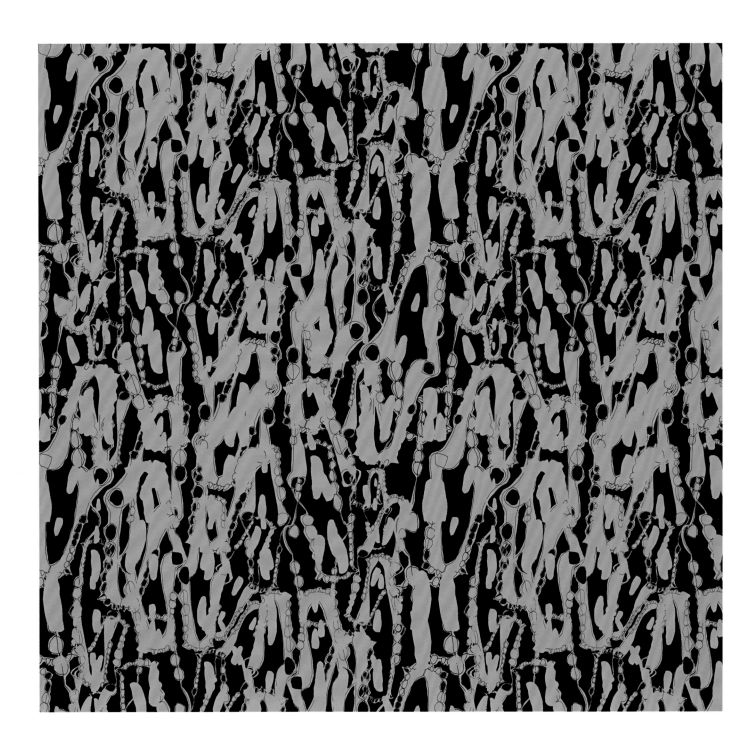

Above -- Based on studies of an animal
jaw-bone, this design shows how a
relatively simple arrangement with
limited colours can become more complex
through the arrangement of the pattern.

Opposite page -- In this printed textile
design from the 'Jaw' collection, the
quality of the drawing and use of colour
clearly communicate Todo Muta's creative
preoccupations.

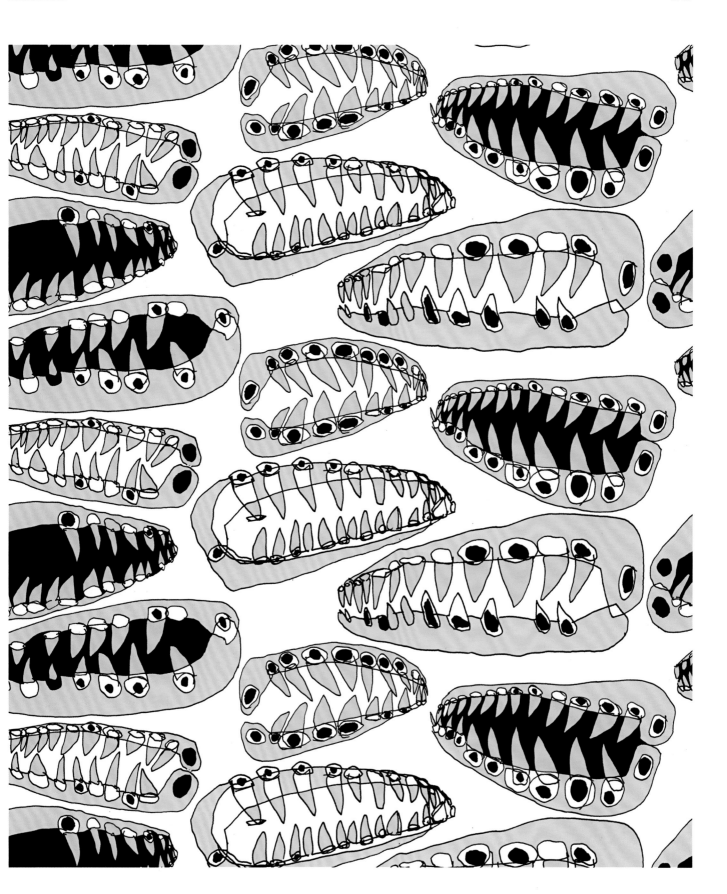

Art

Contemporary artists working with print and pattern are experimenting with new technologies and methods in fascinating and original ways. In the work of Rupert Newman, for example, we see patterns that started out in the form of printed textiles evolve and mutate to become large-scale exterior light projections. Nevertheless, despite the important role played by new media and technologies, it is evident that traditional tools and methods still apply: the art of drawing persists in the animations of Brigitte Zieger, and Sally Greaves-Lord retains historic craftmaking elements in her hand-painted and printed textiles. The rules and conventions are not abandoned, but rather reconfigured to allow space for experimentation and innovation. As we have seen in each section of this book, art and design continue to exert a powerful influence on one another.

The work featured here reflects the varied concerns of artists in the twenty-first century, from their innermost preoccupations to their response to wider global issues. While Ainsley Hillard explores memories from the past in her multi-disciplinary installations, allowing glimpses of something not quite attainable, Francesco Simeti's site-specific pieces illustrate his social and cultural interests, blending historic utopian references with often violent, thought-provoking visuals taken from contemporary media. Los Angeles artist Jim Isermann, meanwhile, draws inspiration from post-war industrial design, Op Art, Supergraphics and mid-twentieth century interior design. conveying utopian ideals through geometry and symmetry.

Liberty Art Fabrics find their way into this part of the book, although they could sit quite comfortably in either of the others. They are included here thanks to their originality, often resulting from unique research trips undertaken by the design team, for example to the subtropical island gardens of Tresco, the catalyst for an original collection of related prints. The diverse activities of architect Richard Weston defy categorization and so fall into this section, as do those of Cristian Zuzunaga, who dexterously moves across a variety of creative domains.

By pushing the aesthetic, technological and artistic boundaries of print, the artists, designers and makers featured here are creating new visual realities and exciting sensory experiences for their audience and consumers. This section illustrates the mutability of print and the broad interpretations and applications that are possible: these creative examples are an exciting, positive foundation and an early sign of things to come in the future. The possibilities seen here suggest that there is no limit to what can be achieved in this field.

Ainsley Hillard

Ainsley Hillard combines an expertise in tapestry-weaving with hand-dyeing, photography, screen and heat-transfer printing to produce remarkable multidisciplinary installation works. Significantly, Hillard's work explores the interface between traditional and new technologies while incorporating a curiosity for experimentation. She explains: 'For me, the fascination of cloth and its construction runs deeper than the physicality of the material itself.' 'In Passing', a seminal piece in her development, highlights her creative interest in the conceptual. Within its woven structures, subtle photographic images provide transitory glimpses of something not quite attainable, a memory of something from the past, something seen on the periphery of consciousness.

'Traces', another key installation by Hillard, at the Mission Gallery, a former seamen's chapel in Swansea, featured 20 suspended hand-woven structures displaying photographic motifs of prayer books, tables and chairs. The motifs were heat-transfer printed on to a viscose weft before being woven through a hand-dyed nylon warp. Original recorded sounds add to the ambience of the space and the resonance of the past. Visitors to the installation were encouraged to move through, around and between the woven images and to engage with the gallery's past. Inspiration was additionally drawn from Cubism, in which objects are not represented from a single focal point. Hillard also explains: 'I wanted to address what [the architect] Juhani Pallasmaa regards as reactivating a peripheral vision and reinforcing haptic experience through the bodily encounter.'

The application of the technique of heat-transfer printing to the weaving process is described in more detail by Hillard: 'The photographic images are heat-transferred on to one side of the weft yarn. The weft yarn is then unravelled and wound on to a shuttle. While the warp width is set at the same width as the photographic image, there is a tendency for the image to shift or become misaligned by the tension of the material during weaving. Each pass of the weft from left to right and vice versa requires the printed side of the weft yarn to be face up, otherwise the image is upside down.' The image will also be upside down if the weft twists, which can happen.

While the photographic images are desaturated, tones of blue and green in the printed weft add their aesthetic to the woven image. Hillard likes black-and-white photography, but she also likes the resulting cool tone of the woven print, which yields an ephemeral, light and airy atmosphere, referencing both the tangible and the intangible.

Hillard uses a plain weave structure, and the density of the cloth is controlled entirely by hand. In some works, such as 'Flow', the weave structure is more open in places to suggest the image emerging through the structure of the cloth. The warp yarn – nylon monofilament – is slippery and as a result relatively difficult to weave. The transparent viscose weft becomes more rigid once printed, and retains its structure once woven. The works are somewhat fragile because of the materials used, and the finished weave can be damaged if the piece is not handled with care.

'Flow' encapsulates the notion of repetition and reflection, through the construction and merging of the figurative image into woven cloth. The installation 'The Window', on the other hand, moves away from the figurative and into interior spaces and objects. Hillard says: 'I am drawn to specific spaces and want to question how we grasp space and place.' 'The Window' captures the essence of a moment and considers the experiential properties of space. Hillard is inspired by the paintings of Vilhelm Hammershøi in her interior and object works, as well as by the writing of Pallasmaa and the philosopher Yi-Fu Tuan on the relationship of humans to their environment. Typically, her projects involve spending a minimum of six months researching the social history of specific architectural spaces and sourcing archival materials to inspire and inform her installations. 'I am interested in materializing the immaterial,' she says. 'I want the viewer to be drawn in to the structure of the fabric, and embrace an embodied and haptic means of looking – to look anew.'

Previous page -- 'In Passing', textile
installation at the John Curtin Gallery,
Perth, Western Australia, 2002.

Above (with details on opposite page) --
'Traces', audio and textile installation
at the Mission Gallery, Swansea, 2008-9.

'For me, the fascination of cloth and its construction runs deeper than the physicality of the material itself.'

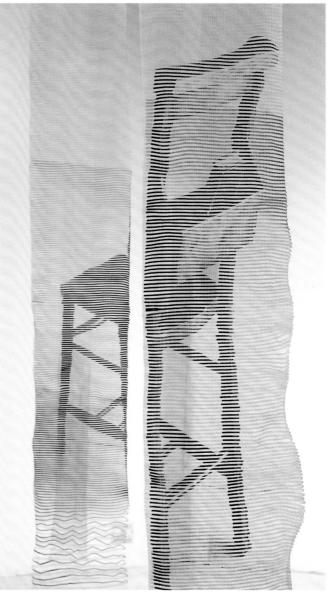

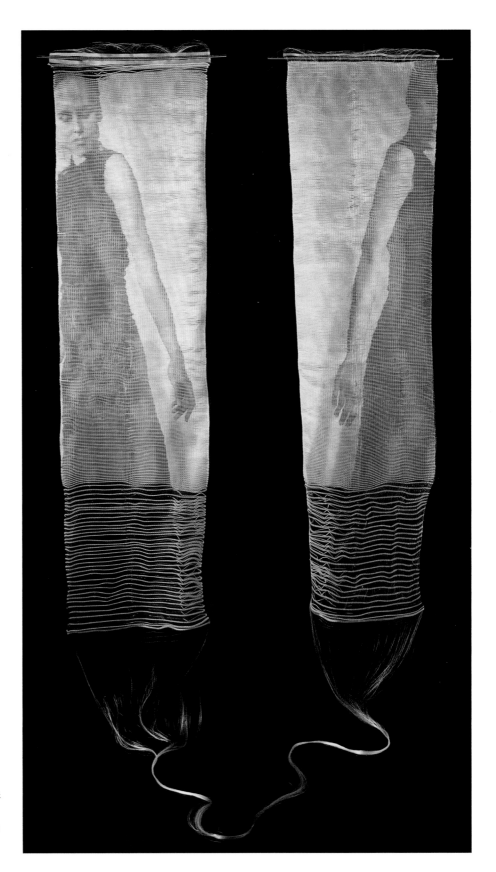

Right (with detail on opposite page) --
'to and fro', 2010. Photographic images
are heat-transferred on to a viscose weft
and then hand-woven through a hand-
dyed nylon warp. 'The act of weaving is
reconsidered, exploring the temporal and
experiential relationship between body,
space and movement,' explains Hillard.

'I am interested in materializing the immaterial ... I want the viewer to be drawn in to the structure of the fabric, and embrace an embodied and haptic means of looking – to look anew.'

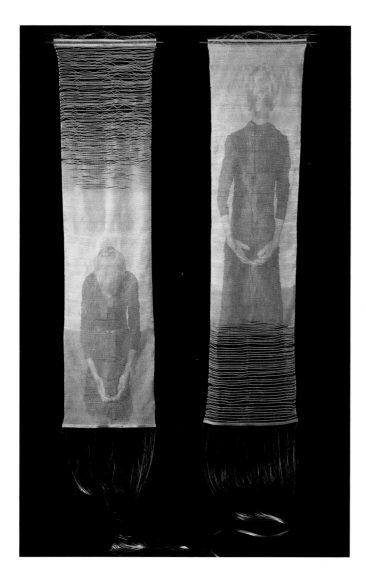

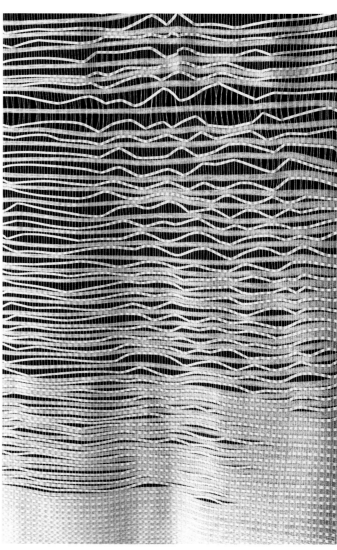

Above (with detail) -- 'Flow', 2012.

Opposite page -- 'The Window', 2013.

Brigitte Zieger

The Paris-based artist Brigitte Zieger creates visual tension by blending historic utopian references with violent, thought-provoking visuals from contemporary society. 'Sometimes it is a kind of obsolete idyllic context that is reassembled with destructive elements,' she explains. 'Other works are related to alternative lifestyles opposed to control and power. Many of my concerns are related more specifically to the role of women inside the historical or political context.' Zieger collects motifs from online sources and press photographs from television news and newspapers to use in her work. She will undermine aesthetic forms and decorative patterns to create pieces that in the first instance suggest harmony, but on closer inspection are full of explosive moments. This is literally the case in the dramatic and dark animation 'Exploding Wallpaper', which speaks about random violence (specific to war), and in which the motifs are erased one by one without any logic.

In her wallpaper-inspired works, Zieger uses traditional toile de Jouy patterns, into which animation is introduced. She chooses the toile pattern for each new piece carefully. For instance, the original toile for 'Shooting Wallpaper' contains the motif of a shepherdess, around which Zieger creates a similarly styled drawing of herself. This drawing becomes the shooting girl animation, and defines the conceptual intention of the piece, the examination of violence and feminine stereotypes.

In 'Tank Wallpaper', violence is ever present. Zieger takes an American tank, the Abraham (active during the war in Iraq), as her central animated motif. The tank moves through a pattern of leafy glade and deer motifs, making a direct reference to hunting.

The print and drawing portrait series 'Women Are Different from Men' represents a move away from wallpaper, although similar conceptual interests persist. Zieger outlines her process: 'For all the portraits the surroundings are erased so as to isolate the figure from her time and place. They are then realized in a mixed technique, based on print and completed with drawing.' In this series it is the image of the armed woman, commonly displayed in the media, that altogether fascinates, seduces and frightens. Zieger uses make-up powder to realize the drawings, and explains: 'I am searching for the place where the viewer gets trapped through a juxtaposition of delicate eye-shadow aesthetics and the disturbing violence of the image.' These gun-aiming women mined from the vast data of the Internet, Zieger explains, 'belong to different geographical and historical zones, different social and political contexts, and build a body of images that questions our collective memory and the more provocative narrative of gender and power.'

The series 'The Eight Most Wanted Women' uses the same techniques and style as 'Women Are Different from Men', but the concept is quite different. Zieger used the FBI's legendary Most Wanted Fugitives list, created to research people considered by the United States to be dangerous. The idea for this piece is certainly informed by Andy Warhol's print series 'Thirteen Most Wanted Men' (1964), but there are differences, most importantly that Zieger's series refers to the women on the FBI list. 'I was curious to know whether there have ever been women on that list,' says Zieger. 'Since its creation 60 years ago, 494 people appeared on the list, but only eight of those fugitives have been women. The first woman to appear on the list was in 1968, a date that coincides with a period of feminism in the USA, when women were demanding greater liberation. The series includes the activist Angela Davis.' Limited to these eight women, the series of print and eye-shadow drawings is adapted from the official photographs used in the 'Wanted' posters.

In the animation 'Bewildered', Zieger incorporates banners from the 1960s to the present day, all collected by her. She also collected nineteenth-century etchings relating to untouched forests from Switzerland to Oceania. The animation travels through these forests, giving the impression of moving from one side of the planet to the other. In this seemingly infinite forest empty of humans, protest banners and placards from bygone demonstrations lie abandoned, the only clue to the presence of humans and to our recent political history.

Zieger's work seems to oscillate between fulfilling the need to create aesthetically desirable artworks and alerting us to the fact that ours is a troubled world full of destruction, alienation and oppression.

Previous page -- In the 'Exploding
Wallpaper' animation (2007), children
play peacefully while explosions take
place at random, progressively erasing
all the patterns (and children).

Above -- 'Shooting Wallpaper', animation,
2006. The motif of the shooting shepherdess
is fashioned on Zieger herself.

Opposite page -- 'Tank Wallpaper',
animation, 2009.

'Sometimes it is a kind of obsolete idyllic context that is reassembled with destructive elements ... my concerns are related more specifically to the role of women inside the historical or political context.'

Opposite page -- Prints with eye-shadow
and glitter on paper, from the series
'Women Are Different from Men', 2011.

Above, left to right -- 'Angela Davis'
and 'Bernardine Dohrn', from the series
'The Eight Most Wanted Women', 2012.
Mixed media drawings with eye-shadow and
glitter on paper.

Above and opposite page -- Stills from
'Bewildered', animation, 2012.

Cristian Zuzunaga

Cristian Zuzunaga was born in Barcelona to a Catalan mother and a Peruvian father, who instilled in him from an early age a curiosity about the world. Zuzunaga is a former student of both the London College of Communication and the Royal College of Art, but before deciding to focus on art and design he was a student of biology, during which time he developed a fascination for the microscope and the magnification of objects. This manifests itself in his creative practice as an interest in the breaking down of images and patterns into minute components.

Zuzunaga's work moves across a number of creative media, including print, photography, textiles and furniture design. When asked if he sees himself as both artist and designer, he says that he does: 'My concepts and initial work tend to come from an artistic process. I am trying to understand the moment we live in and to visualize it through the work I create. Art lifts me and design grounds me. They are complementary practices that inform each other and in my case allow each other to exist. I need both in order to explain my findings and discoveries. One is about multiplicity, the other about uniqueness.'

Zuzunaga goes on to explain another core source of inspiration: 'I use architecture and the way a city is constructed to understand today's present reality. For obvious architectonic reasons, our urban environment is constructed and divided using recurring shapes and forms – mainly squares and rectangles – forming grids and patterns.' Zuzunaga explains an idea that developed while he was studying typographic design at London College of Communication: 'I discovered letterpress, and through it its endless links with architecture … Since then I have been working only with squares and rectangles to construct a strong visual narrative that has its own powerful and versatile style.' This has opened numerous creative possibilities, which have enabled him to see endless links with digital technology, with the pixel at its core, as well as with architecture.

Following a collaboration with the fashion designer Peter Maxwell Smith, in which Zuzunaga designed printed textiles, he was approached by a client to apply his prints to a sofa. He contacted Ron Arad for advice, and Arad directed him to Moroso UK. The result of this chain of events was 'Pixelated', a special-edition printed fabric upholstered on to a Springfield two-seater sofa designed by Patricia Urquiola.

As part of a collaboration with the French furniture designer Christophe Delcourt, in the first instance Zuzunaga presented his 'Pixel' collection to Delcourt, who selected one of the designs for manufacture as a printed textile to be applied to various pieces of furniture. Zuzunaga explains his starting-point for the 'Pixel' collection: 'I always start with a photograph, mainly from the urban landscape. I start to zoom in to break down the image into its infinitesimal components, pixels. Although the urban landscape may appear largely grey, it is in fact composed of millions of colours so small that they are imperceptible to the naked eye. The "Pixel" collection aims to transform our perception of our environment by transforming dull, grey cityscapes into an explosion of colour. … I was involved in every part of the process besides printing, which was done by Kvadrat in Denmark.' The print was upholstered on to sofas and beds from Delcourt's range. The textile was developed so that it would achieve the right balance between the pattern of the fabric and the form of the product.

Zuzunaga displays all the signs of an intellectual designer, as can be seen in his attitude to colour. He explores and designs with colour to stimulate positive emotional responses, which can counteract negative ways of seeing and thinking. His mindset draws on Eastern and Western philosophy as well as alchemy, anthropology and sociology. The psychology of Carl Jung and the concept of the individuation of the soul – a process of psychological integration whereby the unconscious is brought into consciousness to be assimilated into the whole personality – are of interest to Zuzunaga and filter into his creative projects and activities.

'My work focuses on the symbiotic relationship that exists between mankind and its urban environment,' Zuzunaga explains. 'I have been looking at the city as a gravitational force that pulls us towards it, creating a multicultural and multidimensional environment that allows a range of relations to be forged.' He sees the city as a means of communication and a means for communication. He is intrigued by the way we navigate the city with a daily route, which creates patterns, one per person, and in how they may fluctuate from day to day. These are invisible patterns, the traces of which can only be felt. He is also fascinated by the fact that urban environments consist of recurring shapes and forms. He recognizes the architectonic reasons – that space is divided into squares and rectangles, forming grids – and he says 'they become our restriction and at the same time our horizon. We are surrounded by the right angle.' This thinking manifests itself graphically in Zuzunaga's printed textiles and fine-art prints.

**'Art lifts me and design grounds me.
They are complementary practices that inform
each other and in my case allow each other
to exist.'**

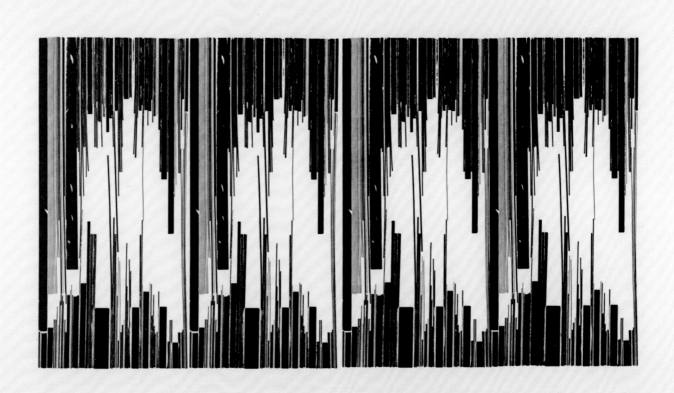

Previous page -- 'Diagonal Chaos',
letterpress. Zuzunaga started using
squares and other geometric shapes when
he discovered letterpress while studying
typographic design. During this time
he also learned about colour-mixing,
hand-printing, detail, texture and the
importance of scale.

Opposite page -- 'Ordering Chaos',
letterpress.

Above -- Digitally printed 'Bitmap' silk
scarves from the 'Alchemy' collection.

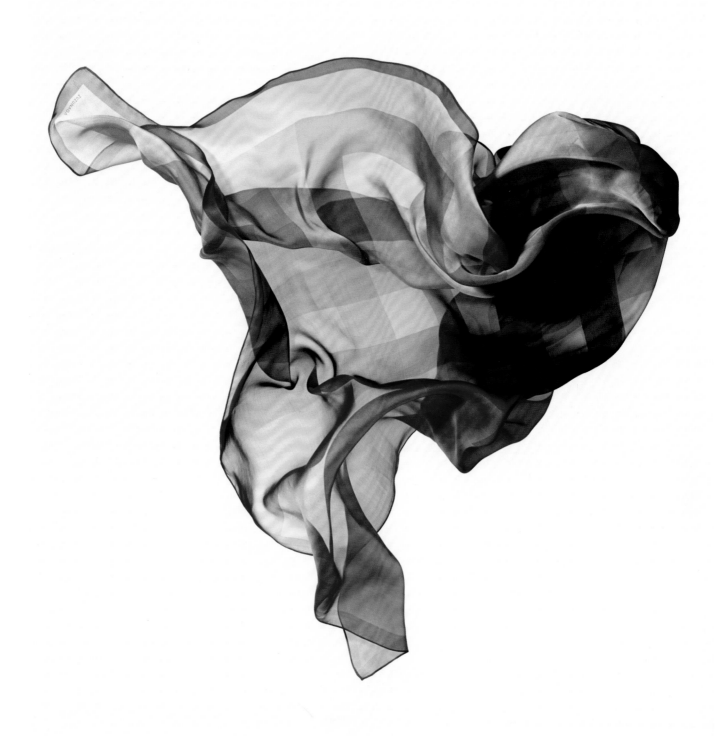

**'My work focuses on the symbiotic relationship
that exists between mankind and its urban
environment ...'**

Opposite page -- 'Giant Flow', digitally
printed silk scarf from the 'Alchemy'
collection. This design started life as
a photograph of the urban environment,
which underwent digital manipulation to be
realized once again in the analogue realm
as a scarf design. This reinterpretation
aims to challenge our thinking about how
an urban environment might be visualized
by a contemporary designer.

Above -- Springfield sofa by Patricia
Urquiola for Moroso UK, upholstered in
Zuzunaga's 'Pixelated' fabric, 2007.

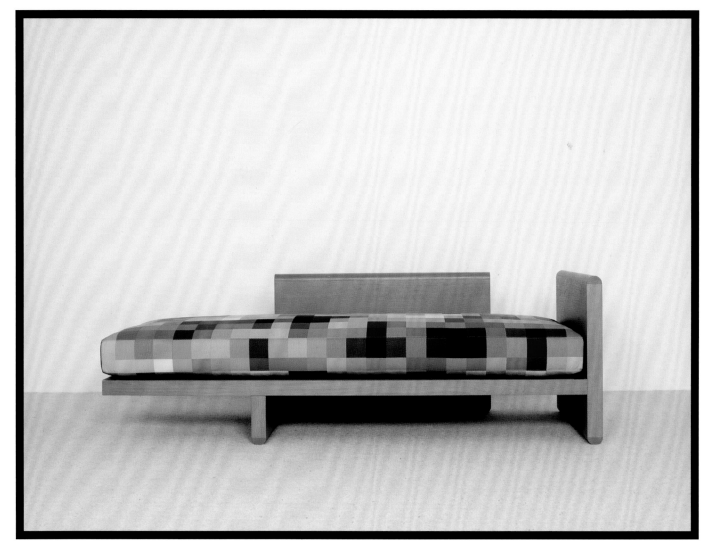

Opposite page, top -- Rue du Jour sofa,
designed by Christophe Delcourt and
upholstered in the special-edition
'Imaginatio' printed fabric by Zuzunaga.

Opposite page, bottom -- NYA Meridienne
daybed, designed as a limited
edition by Vincent Dupont-Rougier,
upholstered in printed fabric designed
by Zuzunaga, and manufactured by
Kvadrat for Christophe Delcourt.

Above -- EOL chairs, designed by
Christophe Delcourt and upholstered in
printed fabric designed by Zuzunaga.

Francesco Simeti

The Italian-born artist Francesco Simeti lives and works in New York and Sicily. Through the use of decorative aesthetics and pattern, he explores provocative themes in installations and site-specific works using digital print on surfaces including wallpaper and glass. His concepts have evolved from such pre-9/11 conflicts as those in Bosnia and Rwanda.

Exhibited at Wave Hill in the Bronx, the wallpaper installation 'Acorn' (2000) gets its name from the acorn pattern in the stucco decoration of the room in which it was installed. The acorn motif becomes a pattern on to which larger motifs of environmental disaster clean-up operations are set in Georgian-style frames to create a set of vignettes suggestive of a not-too-distant future.

'Astro' (2006) again illustrates Simeti's concerns for the future of the planet. It blends elements from children's wallpaper of the 1950s, a time when the race into space echoed Cold War rivalries, with comic-book elements and contemporary images of real explosions taken from the media. Ironically, when this piece was created, United States President George W. Bush was pushing to build the 'Space Shield', which many observers believed would bring the world to a second Cold War.

The following year, Simeti developed 'Kitenge' for the Palazzo delle Papesse in Siena, Italy. This piece drew on dozens of photographs from the genocide in Darfur, in which the refugees' brightly coloured clothing called kitenge appears to be the only visible signifier of a horrifying and seemingly ignored conflict.

'Bensonhurst Gardens', installed in 2012 at a subway station in Brooklyn, draws on a landscape dotted both with plants native to America and plants that are culturally meaningful to the three main ethnic groups that have settled in Bensonhurst. The rose and the lily, for instance, are associated with Santa Rosalia, who is exuberantly celebrated on her name day by Italians in the area. Simeti elaborates: 'While I tend to research my projects meticulously, I do not intend the final piece to be immediately recognizable as about one culture or another; rather, I use these cultural references as a framework.' The overall effect tends towards the surreal: plants are part photographed, part represented by illustrations from different times or cultures. The various species belong in different habitats and cannot be seen together in real life. Simeti reveals that, 'on taking a closer look, the viewer discovers that the soil is indeed an accumulation of waste and generally degraded environment. While this awkward if luscious environment speaks about the perils of our twisted relationship with nature, there is an underlying hope that nature and beauty can and will ultimately prevail.'

The wallpaper installation 'Hillside', exhibited at the Wunsch Ordnung show in Basel, Switzerland, grew out of the same preoccupations as 'Bensonhurst Gardens'. It creates a landscape that represents two different cultural ideas of nature in history and art history, a utopian vision combined with contemporary landscape photographs from the media portraying degradation and pollution. Photographs of clouds, paintings of clouds by European and Eastern masters and photographs of smoke from wild fires and explosions create visual ambiguity.

A collaboration with the innovative furnishing fabric manufacturer Maharam resulted in the creation of 'New World', which was first exhibited at the VitraHaus in Weil am Rhein, Germany, in 2010. Simeti explains his idea for the piece: 'In this digital collage, images are scanned and then elaborated in Photoshop, which is what I use in my printmaking and collages. I am interested in the idea of a repeat that is not too obvious. My goal was to come up with something between a repeated pattern and a wallpaper landscape à la Zuber [the French manufacturer], where the flowers and twigs used as backdrops for John James Audubon's 'Birds of America' prints [1827–38] are extrapolated and become a fictional vine that serves as a grid for a number of plastic hunting decoys, providing an ironic comment on how technological interventions dilute mankind's experience of nature.'

'Tumbleweed' (2010) was conceived in collaboration with the sculptor Andrea Sala as an installation commissioned by the Italian furniture manufacturer Moroso for its showroom during the Milan Salone Internazionale del Mobile of that year. In this installation, Simeti and Sala wanted Moroso's furniture to serve as seating as well as landscape. For them both, travel – as both romantic imaginary journey and path through place and memory – is of interest, but they explain that their thoughts were triggered by actual references, from 'travel in the literal sense, rooted in the landscapes of New Mexico and Texas. That scenery dotted with cacti, saguaros and tumbleweed, the bush that you always see rolling endlessly through Western films.'

'I do not intend the final piece to be immediately recognizable as about one culture or another; rather, I use these cultural references as a framework.'

Previous page -- 'Astro' wallpaper (detail). In this design, Simeti blends elements from 1950s comic books with imagery related to the race into space and Cold-War rivalries between America and Russia.

Opposite page -- 'Acorn' wallpaper (installation view and detail). Here Simeti explores themes of environmental disaster and the subsequent clean-up operations.

Above -- In the conceptual 'New World' wallpaper, plastic hunting decoys inhabit vines, providing an ironic comment on how technological interventions dilute mankind's experience of nature.

Above -- In the installation 'Kitenge',
brightly coloured fabrics act as a
conduit into a conceptual piece aimed at
raising awareness of the largely ignored
Darfur genocide.

Opposite page -- 'Hillside' blends
a utopian historical landscape with
contemporary photographs taken from
the media portraying degradation and
pollution.

Opposite page -- 'Bensonhurst Gardens',
panel sets and installation view at a
New York subway station. The piece
combines plants native to America and
plants that are culturally meaningful to
the ethnic groups settled in Bensonhurst.

Above -- 'Tumbleweed' panels capture the
landscape of New Mexico and Texas, with
cacti, saguaros and tumbleweed.

Jim Isermann

After completing his Master's in Fine Arts in the late 1970s at the California Institute of the Arts, Jim Isermann settled in Palm Springs, California, and became one of a number of second-generation Los Angeles artists. During the high point of postmodernism, Isermann explored neglected and unpopular modernist themes, specifically from the West Coast of the United States, and caught the attention of the art world. His work, which is abstract and occasionally functional, examines the exchange of visual information between high art and postwar industrial design. While his influences include Op Art, Supergraphics and mid-twentieth century interior design, there is a hint of the Renaissance architect in Isermann, reflected in the geometry, symmetry and proportion of his creative style.

Isermann's work conveys a utopian ideal that is local, domestic, personal and of the moment – a place we might inhabit. His output is liberal and democratic, enabling a fluid interchange between art and popular design. He explores and applies notions of migration and appropriation, modifying the aesthetics of Bridget Riley, Donald Judd and the Abstract Classicists John McLaughlin and Frederick Hammersley to utilitarian modern design. Isermann combines a minimalist industrial colour palette with an economical use of materials, displaying Bauhaus tendencies.

Isermann's domain of creative production embraces a broad field of creative media, including die-cut vinyl pattern installations, hand-woven rugs and fabric-covered sculptural cubes as well as painting, drawing and screen printing. His starting-point is often a primary modular unit from the large pool of modern design icons, combined with a small number of industrial colours. For walls and floors, he elaborates these elements through a set of simple algorithmic permutations to generate a pattern of maximum interest and complexity. 'Vinyl Smash Up' (2007), an exhibition of Isermann's die-cut vinyl decals at the Deitch Projects gallery, New York, displayed six different vinyl pieces made between 1999 and 2007. Working with the subtle variations in shape and light of the gallery walls, and its various levels, Isermann adapted his designs to create a dynamic choreography of space. His decals gave form to the wall surfaces by means of colour, pattern, reflection and various other haptic and optic qualities. The bright pop palette and simple forms gave the impression that the patterns were free from the wall. Isermann elaborates on the show: 'All the decal projects [in "Vinyl Smash Up"] were originally created for specific sites … "Vega" (1999) is a six-shape, six-colour decal designed for the approximately 10,000 square feet of wall space at the Le Magasin contemporary art centre, Grenoble, France. The competing patterning of colour and shape never exactly repeats itself. … Most of the decal pieces in "Vinyl Smash Up" have been exhibited in venues in addition to their original specific sites.'

Isermann outlines the creative and practical thinking behind his vinyl wall installation at Art Basel in Miami Beach, Florida: 'It is one decal in two colourways with multiple orientations … based on creating a single three-colour decal that simply through various orientations could create several patterns. The work was produced in two different colourways: red, orange and yellow, and pink, orange and green.' A vinyl pattern from the Art Basel event was also installed in its pink, orange and green colourway in the Edythe and Eli Broad Lobby of the Museum of Contemporary Art in Los Angeles; it was chosen to resonate with the aesthetic of Arata Isozaki, the architect who designed the museum.

Drawing plays an important role in the development of Isermann's projects, as he explains: 'The drawings are most often efforts to solve ongoing problems, such as how to organize repeats for a particular site, scale or dimension. I often see the colour assignment as a description of three-dimensional space, or representative of transparent layers.'

Much of Isermann's work stems from basic, pragmatic problem-solving. The vinyl decals were born out of the simple problem of how to ship works to European shows and not require them to be returned, and they followed a decade of laborious handmade studio works. They were also his first works both to utilize a computer to plot out the repeats and installation schematics, and to be commercially produced. 'Technically', Isermann explains, '… the colours are printed on white vinyl, allowing nearly any colour choice. And because there are many multiples of each shape, a thermal die is made and the decals are stamped out. … When sold, the collector owns the individual pattern, although only one installation may be realized at a time.'

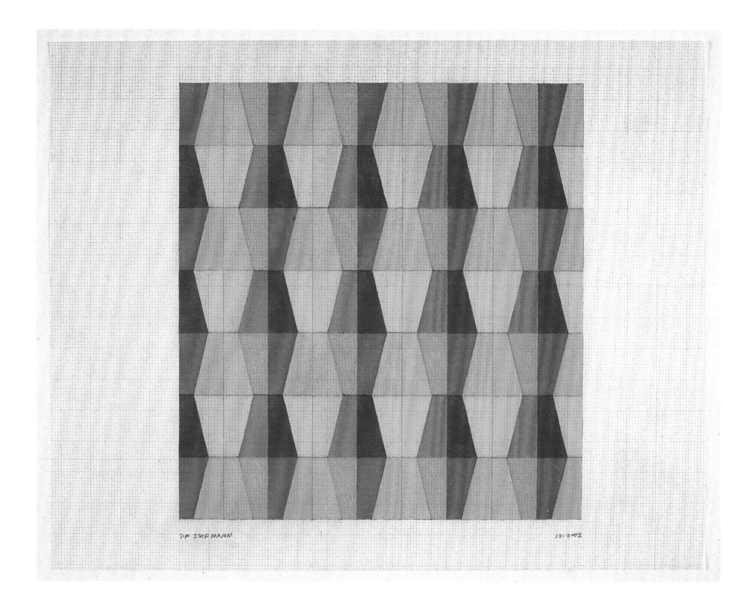

Previous page -- Untitled (0300), die-
cut vinyl decal from 'Vinyl Smash Up',
originally installed at Richard Telles
Fine Art, Los Angeles, 2000.

Above and opposite page -- Geometrical
patterns drawn on graph paper show
Isermann's fascination with twentieth-
century design along with the influence of
Californian artists John McLaughlin and
Frederick Hammersley and their formalist
precedents in abstract art.

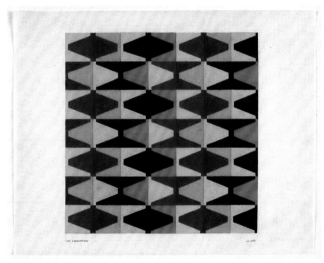

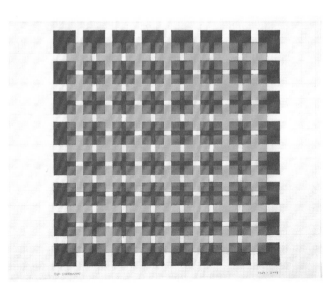

Isermann's work conveys a utopian ideal that is local, domestic, personal and of the moment – a place that we might inhabit.

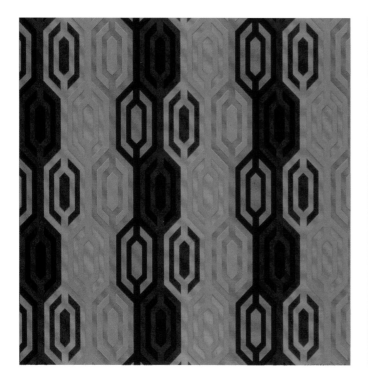
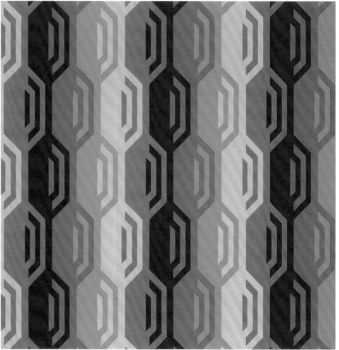

Above -- Two untitled silk-screen prints from a set of three made for Cirrus Editions and Gallery, Los Angeles, 2002. Isermann notes that, 'they are actually not the same design. Each one has a decidedly different type of repetition, although related in geometric structure.'

Opposite page -- Digital print made in 2010 in collaboration with Universal Limited Art Editions to create a limited-edition print in honour of the 150th anniversary of the Albright-Knox Art Gallery, Buffalo, New York. Informed by original paintings, the print captures the essence of Isermann's creative thinking in its vibrant geometry and mathematical precision, reflecting his interest in the intersection of abstract art and industrial design.

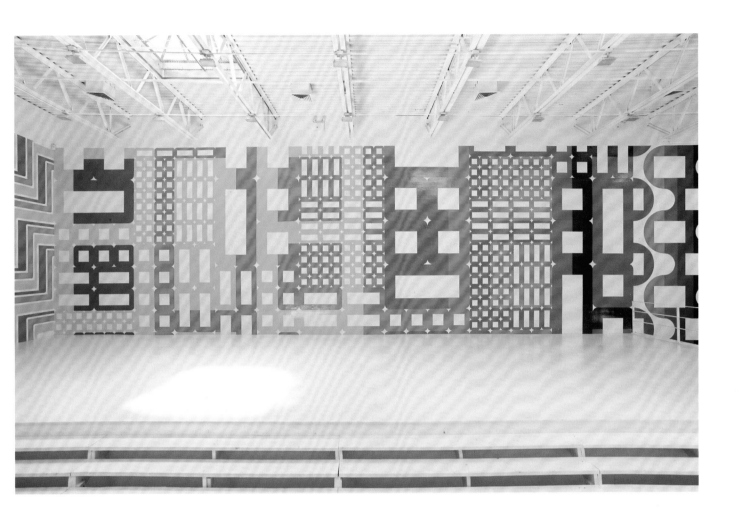

Opposite page, left -- 'Vega' (0299), die-
cut vinyl decals from 'Vinyl Smash Up',
installed at Le Magasin, Centre National
d'art contemporain, Grenoble, 1999.

Opposite page, right -- Die-cut vinyl
decals installed by the Praz-Delavallade
Gallery at Art Basel, Miami Beach, 2010.

Opposite page, bottom -- Untitled (0600),
die-cut vinyl decals from 'Vinyl Smash
Up', originally installed at Praz-
Delavallade Gallery, Paris, 2000.

Above -- Untitled (0699), die-cut vinyl
decals from 'Vinyl Smash Up'.

Katja Davar

The work of the Cologne-based artist Katja Davar is unique, instinctive and highly orchestrated. It conveys surreal worlds through analogue and digital techniques, including printmaking, embroidery and animation, underpinned by drawing and graphite tools. Davar combines metaphors, symbols, scientific and art-historical references to portray the complexity of the world around her, realized through drawing and a fine sense of design.

In Davar's black-and-white animated film 'Grammar' (2010), the scene is a vast snowy landscape with mountainous clouds on the horizon. Fluttering in the wind are flags, adapted from an advertisement campaign by the luxury-goods manufacturer Hermès in which scarves are arranged in a similar way to Tibetan prayer flags. The film blends ideas of spirituality, exoticism, consumerism and the ceaseless spread of technology. The 37 redesigned flags retain a sense of prayer flags but instead of displaying messages from Tibetan deities, each is printed with geometric patterns of circuit diagrams and circuit boards, which nevertheless possess an element of ornamentalism.

This interest in the technical control systems that organize contemporary society is a recurring theme in Davar's work. The juxtaposition of pictorial traditions with the use of technology contributes to the spatial and surreal atmosphere of 'Grammar'. In the film, spiritual symbols are replaced by technological symbols to identify technology as a new religion. Davar explains the ideas behind the piece: 'Circuit systems have always been really important to me as a kind of technological, cartographical "coded" system. By using these ink drawings as textures on the Hermès scarves … I was trying to indicate or "implicate" a different set of values depending on the culture in which one lives.'

The background for the animation 'It's Politics! It Must Be – Such Optimism!' is partly inspired by a stadium designed by the Italian architect Renzo Piano. In this animation, elements of the building are destroyed and the arena is empty apart from a kite attached to rubble on the ground. Around the stadium blows a striped flag displaying a seating plan of the Teatro degli Arcimboldi on the outskirts of Milan, the temporary residence of La Scala opera from 2001 to 2004. The seating plan is repeated three times to form the shape of a fan. The flag and kite react to sounds that the audience can't hear, and to an event which the audience can't see. Davar explains her thinking: 'What interested me in making this work was the idea of changing the context of "culture". A survey was carried out of how the opera-going public changed considerably [when the opera house moved]. When it was situated on the outskirts of Milan, they found that many more students and less well-off people attended … the location made the opera more accessible to people from other backgrounds than the normal La Scala opera public. By using the seating plan but cutting it up, so to speak, in "blocks", I tried to show this compartmentalizing of a "public's" idea of location as not only an architectural/locational issue but also a social issue.'

Both with the kite and flag in 'It's Politics! It Must Be – Such Optimism!' and the flags in 'Grammar', an interesting trompe-l'œil effect occurs through the magic of animation: the motifs and symbols on the kite and flags appear to be printed on fabric, when in reality that is not the case.

The inspiration for the drawing 'That Old-Fashioned Sunset' came in part from the mountainside landscape in Benozzo Gozzoli's fresco Three Wise Men (c. 1460), in the Magi Chapel of the Palazzo Medici Riccardi in Florence. In Davar's reworking, the joyful and vibrant procession of the three wise men is replaced by fundamental, politically sensitive representatives of our time. A power station is positioned dangerously close to a cliff-edge. A pencil sketch in the sky shows the proposed Nabucco natural-gas pipeline from Turkey to Austria, an attempt to reduce Europe's dependency on Russian energy. The rival gas pipeline project led by Gazprom is drawn over the Nabucco line. Wealth charts on the left of the artwork and on the top of the rocky mountainside are printed with a stamping block showing a scatter plot, an abstract indicator of the spread of Western collateral in the past ten years. The work's title is taken from an essay by Oscar Wilde, 'The Decay of Lying' (1909), in which he wrote: 'Nobody of any real culture … ever talks nowadays about the beauty of a sunset. Sunsets are quite old-fashioned.'

Previous page -- The print 'Circle
Time Circle' is explained by Davar:
'It is about a traffic system operating
without an intelligent component,
resulting in the traffic having to halt
for hours, for example in the middle of
the night, although there is no other
car in sight. It is the interpretation
of the logic of a circuit system in
a graphical form, like a topological
bird's-eye view of a system. The title
comes from the green and red traffic-
light phases. The nodal points are
where the traffic stops and the curves
are the movement of the traffic.'

Opposite page -- In the animation
'Grammar', flags printed with circuit-
board imagery are arranged to evoke
Tibetan prayer flags, suggesting
technology as a new religion.

Right -- A kite and flag swirl around
an empty stadium in the animation 'It's
Politics! It Must Be – Such Optimism!'.

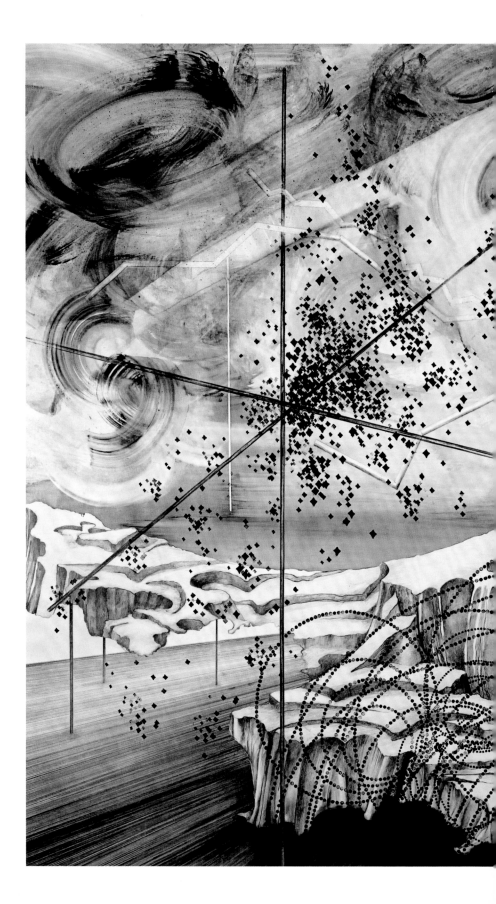

Right -- 'That Old-Fashioned Sunset',
pencil and enamel on paper, 2010.

Davar combines metaphors, symbols, scientific and art-historical references to portray the complexity of the world around her.

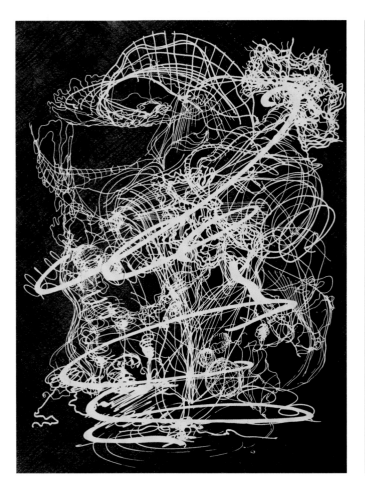

Opposite page -- 'We the Traders',
silk-screen prints. This series of
dark silk-screen prints fed into a
series of works about tulip-mania
in seventeenth-century Holland.

Above -- 'Tomorrow's Giants Today', drawing
and partial print. This work is about
Russia's Gazprom, an extractor of natural
gas and one of the largest companies in the
world. Rem Koolhaas's unsuccessful design
submission for Gazprom's new headquarters is
flanked by a tumbling mountain range of 'peak
oil' 3D diagrams representing the estimated
oil resources remaining in the North Sea.

Liberty Art Fabrics

In 1875 Arthur Liberty opened the now iconic Liberty shop in London, and soon afterwards the company manufactured its first printed silks. In 1904 the company took over a print-works that specialized in block-printed silks, up-river from William Morris's print-works in Merton, south-west London. From the designs and samples printed there was born the extensive Liberty archive, which is now an important resource for designers.

Arthur Liberty had a clear business philosophy, the essence of which is summed up in these words of his: 'I was determined not to follow existing fashions but to create new ones.' This outlook has served the company well, and persists at Liberty Art Fabrics. Typical of this thinking are recent print collections including the 'Guerrilla Gardening' designs, inspired by the loose global movement of that name which encourages gardening without boundaries, bringing life to neglected spaces. Emma Mawston, head of design, outlines the inspiration behind these fabrics: '[Guerrilla Gardening] is a movement I have always loved, as it reminds me of creating art on blank canvases. … The design team visited the incredibly inspiring Richard Reynolds [founder of Guerrilla Gardening], who took us on a tour of his local plantings. Each design was inspired by this trip, the location, Elephant & Castle, the annual sunflower planting, the amazing lavender roundabout and a cityscape of London representing the British arm of this organization.' The print design 'Richard and Lyla' depicts Richard Reynolds and his wife, who met while planting tulips on a London roundabout. 'Castile' represents the Elephant & Castle Urban Forest campaign of summer 2011, which was organized to regenerate this area of London and to save trees. The 'Mayrose' design, meanwhile, refers to the annual event in May in which Guerrilla Gardeners all over the world plant sunflowers.

The 'Botanical Gardens' collection of digital prints is principally the result of an inspirational field trip by the design team to the subtropical garden at Tresco Abbey on the Isles of Scilly. The collection includes designs by the eminent artists Mary Fedden, Hugo Grenville and Rachel Pedder-Smith.

The motto inscribed above the iconic Secession building in Vienna, 'To the age its art, to art its freedom', symbolizes the the vision of the Secessionist art movement under the leadership of Gustav Klimt, who inspired eminent painters, architects and designers. This reactive movement instigated a shift in the perception of Vienna as an avant-garde creative centre. A research trip to Vienna by the Liberty Art Fabrics studio resulted in a series of highly decorative print designs displaying characteristics of Viennese art nouveau, such as 'Gustav and Otto', referring to Klimt and the architect Otto Wagner, and the complex 'Reuben Nouveau'.

Mawston is keen to point out that the vibrant creative culture at Liberty Art Fabrics is not new: 'I have been pushing the boundaries of print techniques and design since I started, as I am sure many in my position have done before me. We are also collaborating with printers who are able to work with us to achieve our desired results and introduce us to new techniques … we now print digitally and with screen so that we can provide the most diverse and interesting collections.'

Mawston recognizes that the fundamental reasons for the ongoing success of Liberty Art Fabrics can be explained by its design philosophy: 'Our philosophy is firstly to work very hard, but love what you do and then your talent will shine through. Hand-drawing and a diverse and inspiring sense of colour are very important. The studio is an equal mixture of structure and Bohemianism. Original briefs and research are central to our design philosophy, as is working as a very tight-knit team. Our customers are global, so listening to their feedback is always important. We work for a British company with a very rich heritage, so we have to create collections with a mix of tradition and experimentation.'

'I was determined not to follow existing fashions but to create new ones.'

Previous page -- 'Archipelago' is one of
a number of designs realized after the
team's visit to Tresco Abbey Gardens on
the Isles of Scilly.

Opposite page -- 'Otilia' conveys a
fantastical forest created through the
digital manipulation of photographs
to portray the magic and diversity of
Tresco Abbey Gardens.

Above left -- 'Abbey Pool' is inspired
by the twentieth-century British artist
Mary Fedden, whose work concentrates on
a preoccupation with still-life with a
view beyond.

Above right -- 'Pointillism' is an
abstract, impressionistic print based on
the wild floral fields of Tresco. Layers
of thickly applied oil paint create a
multicoloured texture.

Above left -- In the 'Mayrose' design from the 'Guerrilla Gardening' collection, large sunflowers are realized through a combination of hand-drawing and crayon layers that are subsequently scraped out.

Above right -- 'Richard and Lyla' from the 'Guerrilla Gardening' collection is inspired in part by a 1950s archive print, reworked and hand-painted to depict Guerrilla Gardeners bringing plants to an urban landscape.

Opposite page -- 'Castile' from the 'Guerrilla Gardening' collection captures wonderful watering machines, sunflowers and wildlife among a diverse range of flora and fauna. There is also a distinctive 'elephant and castle' motif.

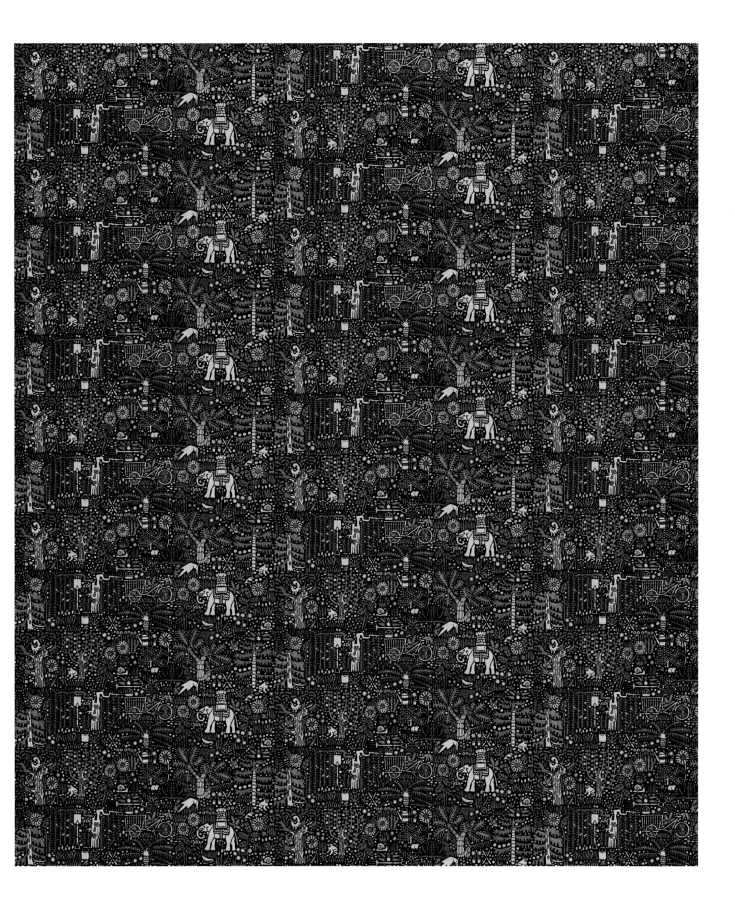

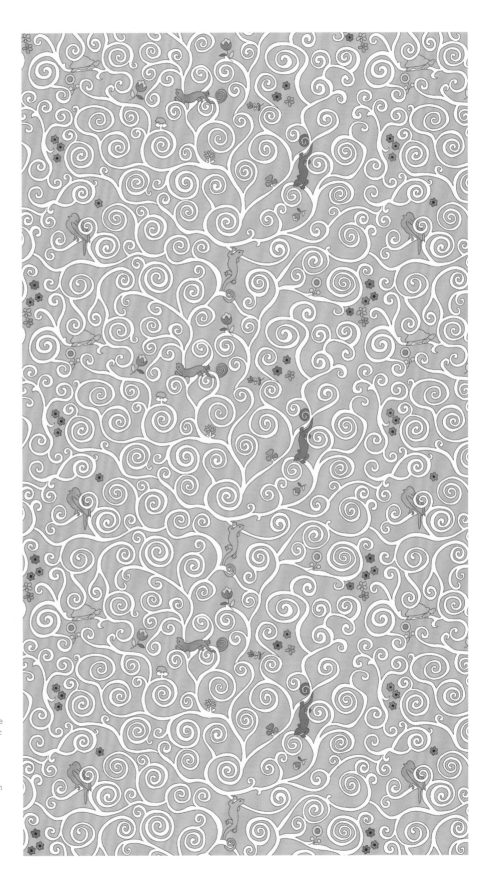

Opposite page -- 'Reuben Nouveau' from the
'Vienna' collection is a complex geometric
watercolour informed by the architectural
details of the Secessionist house in
Vienna and the paintings of Gustav Klimt.

Right -- The design 'Gustav and Otto' from
the 'Vienna' collection displays a spiral
pattern inspired by Klimt's paintings,
blended with small sculpted creatures
from the buildings of Otto Wagner.

Peter Pilgrim's work as an artist and designer started seriously at the Royal College of Art in London in the late 1960s, when his practice was informed by developments in the Op Art movement. He equally admires minimalist artists such as the sculptor Donald Judd, and the early work of Frank Stella. These early associations and influences have informed the conceptual and aesthetic identity of Pilgrim's work over time. But he has also drawn inspiration from iconic twentieth-century designers and movements: 'I am influenced by the Bauhaus and the wonderful woven fabrics of Jack Lenor Larsen, the knits of Missoni and the jazz prints of Bernard Nevill [former design director of Liberty].' Pilgrim's more recent encounters with the creative realms of digital design and technology have resulted in creative outcomes that seem to echo and resonate with the simple yet rich work of these artists and designers. Pilgrim, however, does not limit himself to these points of reference; he also holds in high regard the leading twentieth-century British painters John Hoyland and Patrick Heron and the American Pop Art movement.

Colour is the essence of Pilgrim's creative practice. 'I nearly always use complementary colour, playing with tone and discord,' he says, 'and I mix this with harmonic colour which, when one colour interacts with another, creates visual illusions that change the tone and intensity of colours depending on what colour is next to what or what colour surrounds another. The whole process is more organic than the finished work would suggest.'

Pilgrim has been involved in a number of art and design projects, most of which started life as very rough sketches that then took the form of paintings or digital artworks. This was the case for the designs 'Shift', 'Arc' and 'Shimmer', which all started life as oil paintings. While they function as statements in their own right, they also underwent a series of digital manipulations before being manufactured using the latest digital print technology at the experienced print manufacturer R.A. Smart in Macclesfield, northern England, where they were transferred on to Habotai silk using acid dyes and made into huge banners in readiness for exhibition. The original paintings were suspended in front of the banners, emphasizing the subtly different scales and slight distortion of the images. The finished project came to fruition in exhibitions at the Atrium Gallery in London and Silpakorn University in Bangkok, the latter opened by the British Ambassador.

'Shimmer' and 'Shift' were used as front-cover images for *International Textiles* magazine, and 'Shimmer' was commissioned by the textile designer Georgina von Etzdorf to be adapted into a series of printed scarves, gloves and slippers. In the process the design was radically reduced in scale and digitally printed, again by R.A. Smart, on to silk, velvet and leather. 'Shift' was used by Susan Benjamin for a series of housewares: luxury photograph albums, small leather trays and address books. Pilgrim explains: 'The title and my name were used on the spines and [the products were] sold online … Both Georgina and Susan Benjamin organized royalty deals with me, which … is almost unheard of in the textile sector.'

'Steps Ahead' started life as another of Pilgrim's original large oil paintings, which was digitally 'tidied up', manipulated into new shapes and repeated using computer-aided design for digitally printed fabrics commissioned for installation in the boardroom of Ravensbourne College of Design and Communication in south-east London. The transformation, preparation and printing were again done by R.A. Smart with instructions from Pilgrim, who explains: 'The really interesting point here is that I [have] developed such a close working relationship with one of [R.A. Smart's] computer technicians that most images I want to create can be talked through over the telephone. I did email them a rough collage of what I wanted though. Also, the colour matching is so good that I rarely have to ask for a strike-off to be sent before the production run.'

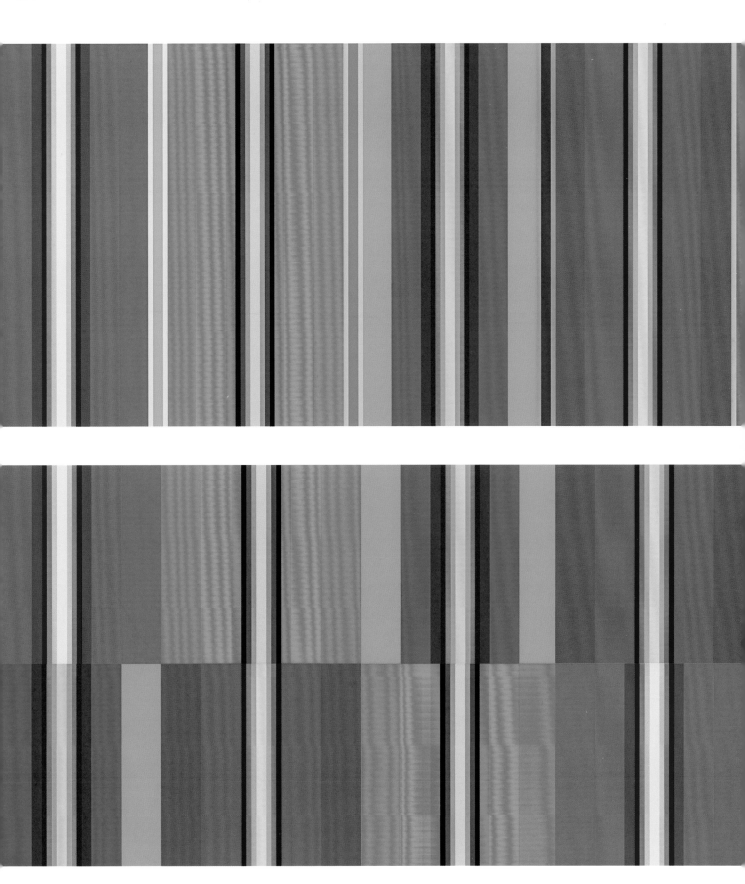

Previous page -- 'Neon', digital design
(top), and in a digitally printed block
repeat (bottom). This design is informed
by the vivid colour and luminescence in
coloured neon light, particularly as seen
in the work of the American artist Dan
Flavin. It was realized using the Adobe
Illustrator program.

Above, left to right -- 'Shift', original
oil painting, and applied to a kimono,
through a collaboration with the Canadian
fashion designer Dianne Taylor.

Opposite page -- 'Arc', original oil
painting.

**'The whole process is more organic than the
finished work would suggest.'**

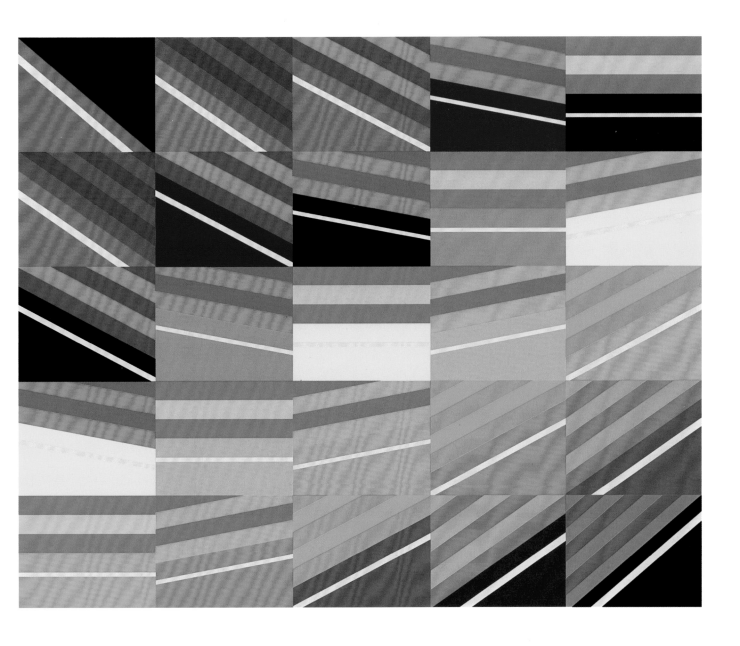

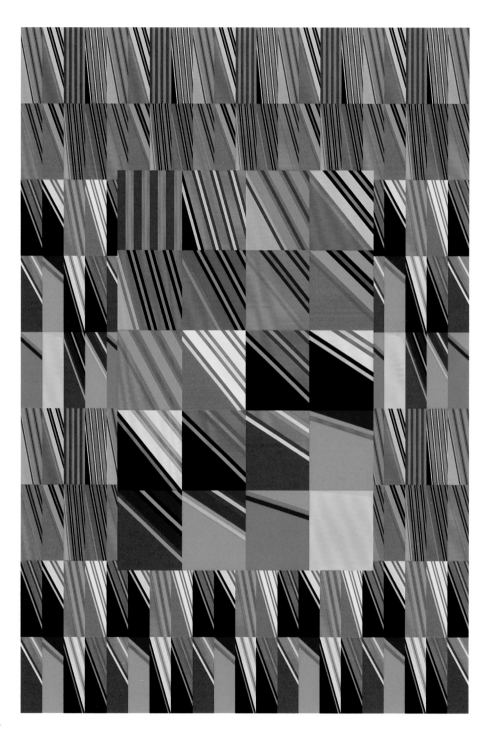

Opposite page -- 'Shimmer', original oil painting. Simple, loosely rendered oblongs cover the whole canvas. While the motifs appear to be randomly placed, they do follow a basic form of mathematical modular progression, providing an intuitive as well as an intellectual approach to the use of colour.

Above -- 'Shimmer', digital inkjet print on Habotai silk. In this digitally manipulated version of the design, the dimensions and scale of the pattern have been significantly reduced to allow greater flexibility in its potential uses.

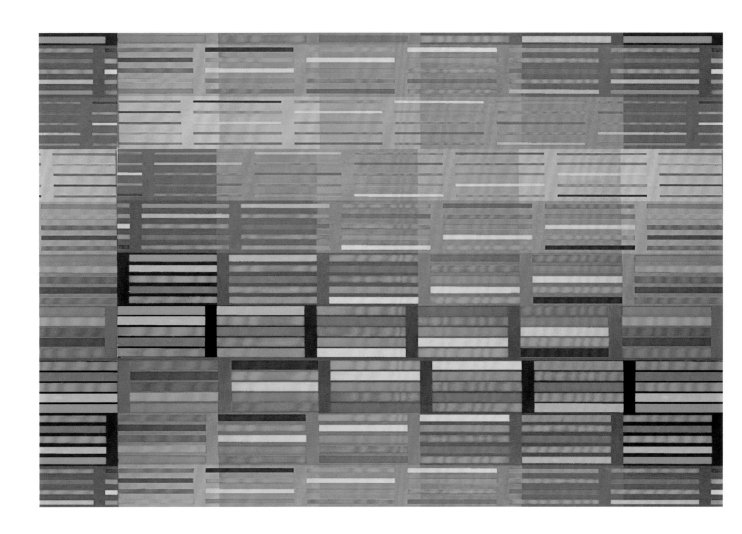

Above -- 'Steps Ahead', digital repeat print
manipulated from an original oil painting.

Opposite page -- The 'Steps Ahead' print
is manipulated further with computer-aided
design to extend the range of shapes and
repeats allowed by the pattern.

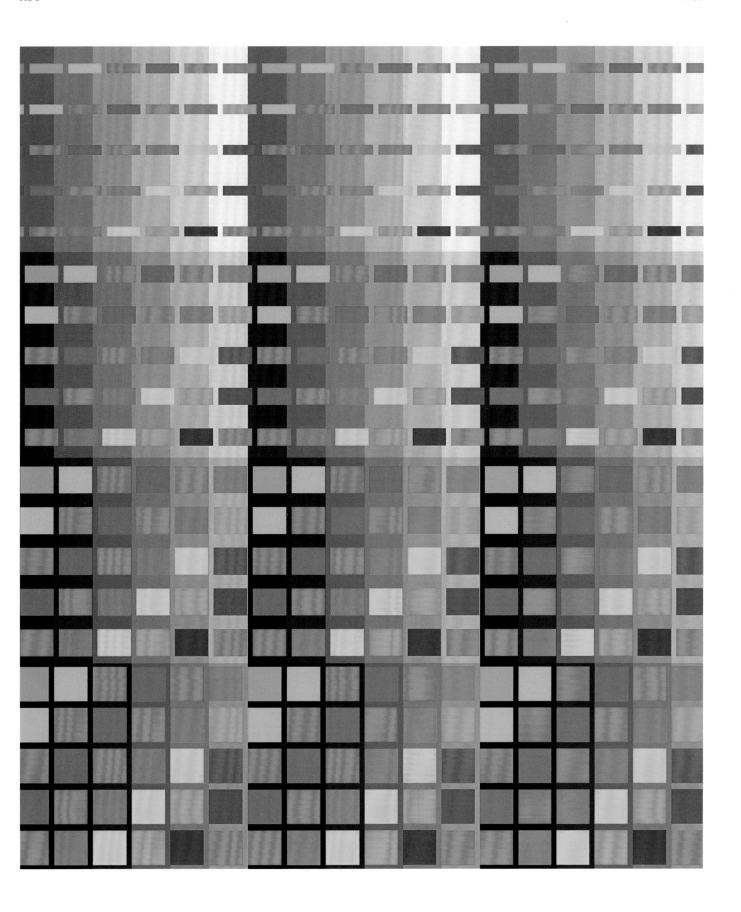

Richard Weston

Professor of architecture Richard Weston began scanning minerals in 2003 after buying his first scanner. Having acquired a beautiful ammonite fossil, he wanted to discover what level of detail it might reveal once scanned. The first results were disappointing, but after buying a high-resolution machine Weston began to see subtle and colourful results. For the next few years he spent his spare time scanning minerals, in what is no passing whim. Weston has a long-standing fascination with natural forms and processes, qualified by bookcases full of related publications. With his scanning technology, he captures natural forms at an architectural scale, presenting fresh examples of what John Ruskin in *Modern Painters* (1843) describes as 'the pure wild volition and energy of creation'.

Not until talking to a friend, who commented on the potential of digitally printing the scanned minerals on to fabric, did Weston consider a commercial application to be worth pursuing. Significantly, he explains: 'Listening to the *Today* programme [on BBC Radio 4], I heard Liberty of London's new American Head of Buying, Ed Burstell, talking about his "open call" for new products. Laid low with a cold, I missed the first event but attended the second – and was delighted to discover that it was being filmed for a BBC2 television series, *Britain's Next Big Thing*.' Burstell loved what he saw, and eighteen months later 'Weston scarves' were Liberty's best-selling brand.

In order to be printed on to silk scarves, the image files needed a lot of 'cleaning'. Apart from the extraneous dust on the scanner, the fine powder used to polish the mineral specimens left its traces. And sometimes, explains Weston, it is necessary to edit such minor flaws as cracks: 'Most of the first few collections of scarves were "straight from nature", but I am willing to manipulate – but only so far as the result seems "natural". That, needless to say, is a tricky call. But it's intriguing how inverting the colours of a file can yield a "new" mineral very similar in colour to a "real" one. There is always a loss of subtlety, of course, and the integrity of the sources has to be respected.'

In collaboration with the architectural firm Patel Taylor, Weston created an agate facade for a house in Camden, north London. Weston outlines the circumstances and processes involved in the project: 'Both partners [of Patel Taylor] are old friends and visiting professors at the Welsh School of Architecture, where I teach. Andy Taylor was fascinated by my new "departure", and suggested the house as a test case. The agate image was massively enlarged and printed as a series of Habotai silk panels. These were then carefully positioned on laminating film between glass and fired in a kiln by a firm called Hourglass. The films are UV light-proof, so the material should be long-lasting, and the edges are sealed with a tiny bead of silicon that will need renewing perhaps every 15 years.'

The phrase 'Digital Arts and Crafts', used by Weston, is more than an implied allegiance with the movement founded by William Morris but, as Weston explains, 'whereas William Morris's ideals were grounded in a reaction against the consequences of mass production for both the quality of goods and the lives of workers, the Digital Arts and Crafts will embrace the new, nimble technology of design and production to enable designer-makers to flourish and to transform customers into clients able to participate creatively in the design of their everyday goods and homes.' Consequently, Weston is now working on digital apps that will enable people to participate creatively in making designs, and he can see an online community developing around this idea. A key aspect of this vision is to promote greater individuality.

Weston's pursuit of the world's most beautiful natural materials created a unique moment in art and design in relation to print. His unconventional thinking has resulted in innovation across a myriad of products, emanating from an initial obsession with no perceived application, transformed through digital techniques into commercial but unique fashion, design and architectural products. No doubt Weston is set to provide further creative surprises, as can already be seen in his preliminary renderings of furniture textiles.

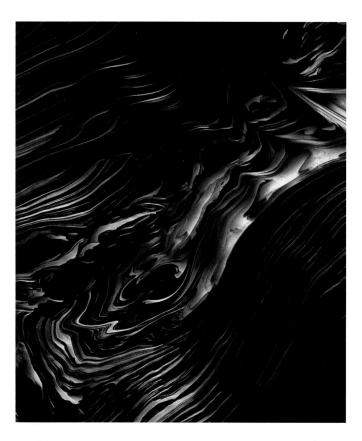

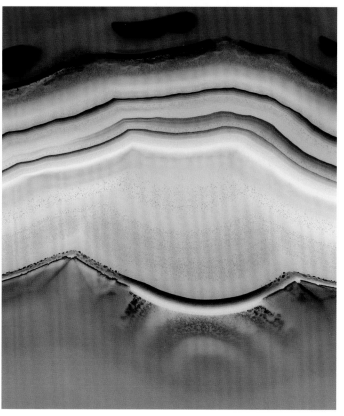

'I am willing to manipulate – but only so far as the result seems "natural".'

Previous page -- A Mexican smoky
fluorite becomes a Weston silk scarf with
remarkable colour combinations caused by
impurities and the mineral's exposure to
radiation as it formed.

Opposite page, clockwise from top left
-- Obsidian, also called volcanic
glass, is created by lava cooling
so quickly that a crystal structure
forms. -- Elestial quartz is the
source material for the 'Wild Quartz'
silk scarf. -- Two different forms of
agate, a microcrystalline variety of
silica (chiefly chalcedony) classically
associated with volcanic rocks, are
scanned with stunning results.

Above -- 'Montana agate' silk scarf
draped over rocks. Montana agate
formed during volcanic activity in
the Yellowstone Park area of the
United States millions of years ago.

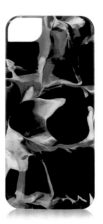

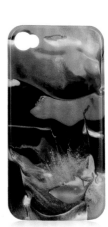

Above -- The mineral mica schist is a
crystalline metamorphic rock with mica
flakes generally parallel in order. Mica
schist in this instance appears in the
design for a large silk scarf.

Above right -- Mobile-phone cases show
the breadth of potential applications
for Weston's mineral motifs.

Opposite page -- Digitally printed
Weston silk scarves on display at
Liberty of London.

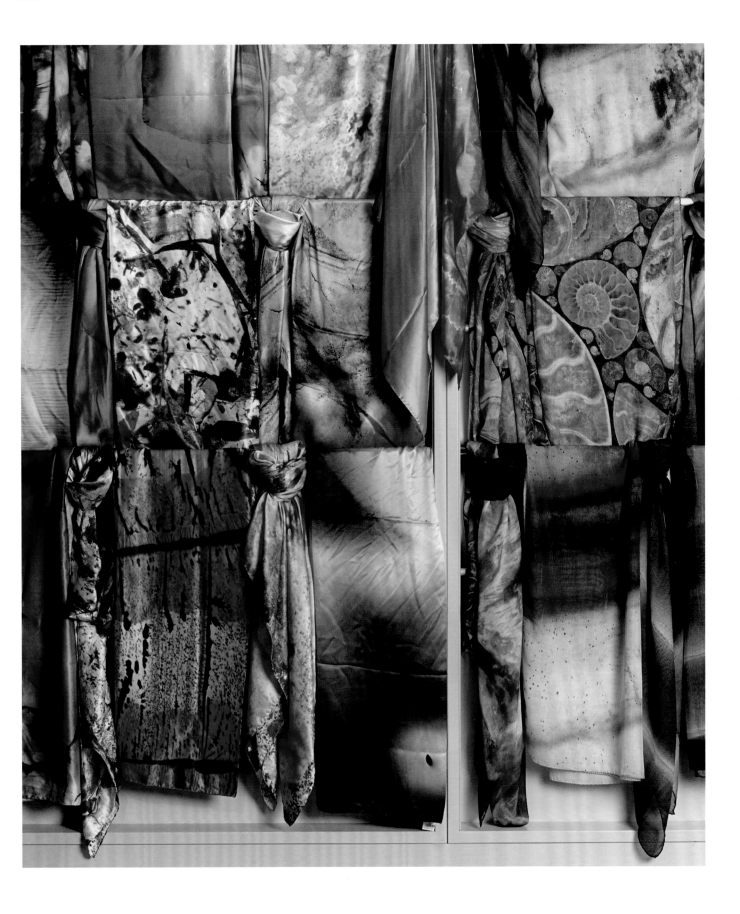

Opposite page -- A collaboration with
the architects Patel Taylor on a house
in Camden, north London, resulted in a
three-storey silk-in-glass agate facade,
inspired by Weston's collection of
minerals, rocks and fossils.

Above -- This rendering of a chair
suggests the potential application of
Weston's mineral designs to furniture.

Right -- Agate tile panel at Johnson Tiles.

Rupert Newman

Rupert Newman traverses the boundaries between art and design with considerable dexterity, a way of thinking and working he articulates simply: 'I work as both a designer and an artist, and the two bounce off each other. I take designs from my art and art from my designs.' This approach has evolved from experience in printed textile design acquired while studying at Falmouth University and the Royal College of Art. Newman's digital designs have featured on textiles in the collections of brands ranging from Giorgio Armani to Gap. Having also worked at the acclaimed digital design studio Circleline in London, Newman is well equipped to develop and apply his knowledge to fashion and interior markets as well as art.

Working principally in the virtual world of the computer, Newman takes full advantage of the opportunities provided by the design tools in Photoshop. In this digital realm he explores the fundamental aesthetic themes of composition, colour and pattern, which evolve from his scanned paintings, and which undergo transformation on the computer. Inspiration for his paintings can come from a variety of sources. For example, in the past designs have developed from sketches of port vineyards in Portugal. Art-historical inspiration is equally important for Newman. He is fascinated by the early twentieth-century art movement Rayonism, named in part for the use of dynamic rays of contrasting colour, which represent lines of reflected light.

These influences are apparent in his abstract patterns and are exemplified in his recent light-projection works. Newman explains: 'These projections stem from paintings, which often evolve into prints or surface patterns. I adapt my surface patterns for projecting, taking it one step further by mapping them to a building and animating them.' Recent venues for Newman's projections include Aboyne Castle in north-eastern Scotland, and the country houses Great Fulford and Ugbrooke House in Devon. He often collaborates with the sound designer Sarah Warne, whose soundscapes provide a vital dimension, adding both suggestion and counterpoint to the experience. Newman works with exclusive party planners to produce his bespoke, original content, which transforms architecture into unique and dynamic canvases for the digital displays.

The projections at Aboyne Castle were the result of his involvement in a wedding party. Throughout the evening, Newman projected an evolving, eye-catching and contrasting selection of designs in varying scale to generate a remarkable visual extravaganza. One of the projected designs, a geometric pattern, illustrates his fascination with Rayonism. Another, circular pattern shows the mutability of his work in its adaptation from a series of his digitally printed textiles called 'Circular Motion'. Newman explains: 'For each project I tailor designs responding to what the client wants, just as I would a textile collection or an art commission. Sometimes I have free rein to do what I want, and other events are more restricted (usually those for more corporate clients).' Newman has also undertaken interior projections, such as 'Corals of the Deep', displayed at an event in the Great Hall at Great Fulford.

While light projections are a current focus for Newman, he continues to design digital prints, which are sold to a number of international fashion houses. He also explores other possibilities for his ideas. This is evident in the striking surfboard design incorporating one of Newman's digital prints on fabric. Newman describes the project: 'It was a relatively simple process. I downloaded a surfboard template, chose a border colour, and went ahead and adapted one of my designs to fit the length of the board. (The original was a painting and collage in my sketchbook.) I wanted to keep the scale big in the middle and small at the tips.'

Newman also holds exhibitions in London at which he sells framed prints. The focal point of one exhibition was a multisensory installation piece, two minutes of sound and projected visuals. Another exhibition featured digital prints with mapped projections but no sound. This is a new concept for Newman, in which specially designed light effects are mapped and then projected in accordance with a framed, static image.

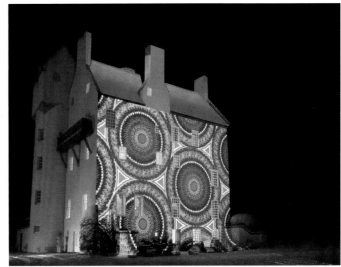

Previous page -- 'Geo-Circular' (detail),
digital repeat print design.

Opposite page -- 'Architectural'
(detail), digital repeat print design.

Above -- Light projections of 'Circular
Motion' and an untitled pattern inspired
by fractured light and smashed glass
at Aboyne Castle (top left and right),
Ugbrooke House, Devon (bottom left), and
Great Fulford, Devon (bottom right).

Above -- 'Corals of the Deep', light
projection in the Great Hall at Great
Fulford, Devon.

Right -- The 'Corals of the Deep'
pattern (detail).

Opposite page -- Here Newman's artwork
is digitally printed on to fabric and
then incorporated into the design of
a surfboard.

'I work as both a designer and an artist, and the two bounce off each other. I take designs from my art and art from my designs.'

Sally Greaves-Lord

Sally Greaves-Lord will not limit her creative outlook, and outlines why: 'Everything I see, hear or feel has its effect. There are of course the things I love, such as the billowing banners in Kurosawa's film *Seven Samurai* [1954], which are etched in my mind. I am drawn to the potent and curious uses of textiles all over the world. My textile interests are many and varied and I do not find myself much interested in how things are made, more in how they are used and the life they have once they are finished.'

Trained in printed textiles, she largely produces her work by masking out areas and hand-painting or printing through a screen over stencils on to cloth, creating striking pieces with bold motifs, strong colours and an acute sense of composition. This imposing style has been applied to site-specific and exhibition work as well as to interior and fashion projects. She draws on varied experience, from a position as creative director at Issey Miyake UK to collaborations with the Conran Group and Durham Cathedral.

Her inspiration is seldom taken directly from a particular place. The exception, she says, is that 'if I have a very specific request for a commissioned piece, I do try consciously to involve motifs, moods, colours and atmosphere of a particular place'. Painting in the landscape, usually at a location with an associated meaning, can inform her new work. Painting indoors is another starting-point for Greaves-Lord, who takes contextual inspiration from the intimate interior paintings of Édouard Vuillard. Intermittently, architecture has been influential, such as the work of the Secessionist architects of Vienna: Otto Wagner, Josef Hoffmann and Joseph Maria Olbrich. Greaves-Lord is also impressed by the sculptural architectural work of Carlo Scarpa.

Colour is fundamental to Greaves-Lord's aesthetic: 'I get a terrific amount of pleasure working with colours … I never plan them in advance, unless for a commissioned work with a particular brief.' Composition is a key aesthetic, too: 'I often think that composition is even more important to me than colour. In fact I do think it is. At least, today I do.' Intrinsic to her focus on composition is the edge of a piece of work, which through her creative process generates a dynamic tension between other compositional elements.

A small black-and-white sketch is the normal starting-place for new work, Greaves-Lord says: 'As I sketch I usually develop a strong impression of what the piece will be like, or what it could be like. I am not certain that it is any more formed than a dream on waking, which seems clear enough until you try to focus on the details. Like a dream, it is more a strong feeling of what the work will be.' When she is immersed in her work, on the cloth, her process grows naturally. Colour and composition develop in their own way, gradually changing with colours drifting into different hues, light and dark and saturation levels fluctuating as influences and sources shift into and out of focus. She makes only decisions she feels certain about, preferring if she is unsure to wait until she knows what to do next.

Depending on the project, Greaves-Lord might do something rash if nothing seems to be moving; if it doesn't work out, she will work over it, not minding about the handle of the cloth. This represents a marked change in her thinking from her earlier work, when it was important that the cloth remain beautifully soft and not overworked, a time when she used only dyes that did not affect the feel of the

silk or cotton. Recent work combines print methods, such as hand-dyed or digitally printed backgrounds with pigment print paste applied to the surface.

The names of her pieces emerge while she is making them, and words and phrases come to mind when she is preoccupied with colour and composition. She says: 'I used to number my works, until I realized that this made the pieces sound somewhat dry and inaccessible. I began to find the thought of naming them rather interesting, and I felt that a title would become part of the work and add a new dimension … I intend my work to be open to the viewer, and the interpretation not to be constrained by the title but maybe excited by it … My works are not "about" one single idea or place, but a whole rounded moment in time.'

Previous page and above -- This
windbreak, designed by Greaves-Lord, was
commissioned for the Sea Swim project
on the North Yorkshire coast, organized
by artists John Wedgwood Clarke and
Lara Goodband. They explain: 'We wanted
something we could use to "draw" shapes
on the low tide beach in a way that people
would notice and that would give them a
sense of scale. We also needed a shelter
and an open-air performance space – the
windbreak solved these needs beautifully.
Without being literal, the design reflects
the sensation of swimming and the
swimmer's perspective on the land.'

Opposite page -- Sea Swim deckchairs
designed by Greaves-Lord, with text by
John Wedgwood Clarke.

**'Everything I see, hear or feel has its effect ...
I am drawn to the potent and curious uses of
textiles all over the world.'**

Opposite page and above -- The printed
wall-hangings 'Clouds', 'Sky', 'Water' and
'Woods' (left to right) are a result of a
Connections North residency in Finland,
which culminated in their exhibition in
Finland and England.

**'My works are not "about" one single idea
or place, but a whole rounded moment
in time.'**

Above -- Designs for printed glass panels
for Bransholme Health Centre in Hull.

Opposite page -- Designs for the
'Celebrating Place' project became
remarkable printed tableware items
inspired by National Trust properties
Nunnington Hall and Rievaulx Terrace
in North Yorkshire.

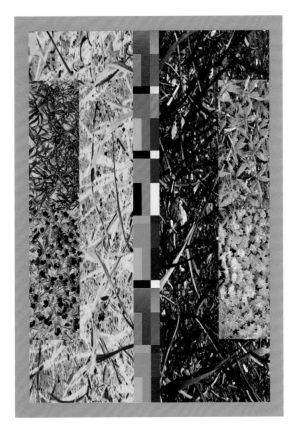

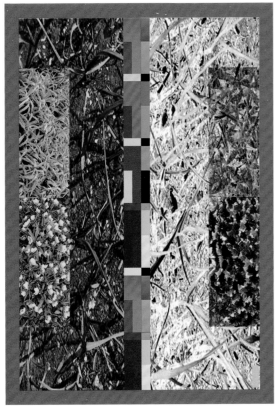
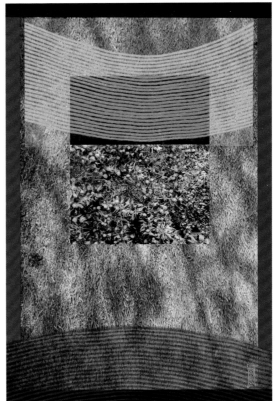

Glossary

Acid dye
A textile dye effective in the dyeing of protein-based fibres such as wool and silk.

Backing cloth
In printed textiles, this is an absorbent cotton cloth applied to the print table before printing lightweight fabrics such as silk and Lycra, which reduces smudging and lack of adhesion during printing.

Block printing
A technique in which ink is applied to a chiselled wood-cut design on a wooden block and then applied to the fabric.

Burn-out printing
See **Devoré**.

Cellulosic fibres
Plant-based fibres such as cotton and hemp.

Colourway
One of several colour solutions for a design.

Computer-aided design (CAD)
Dedicated design software used partially or wholly in the generation of a design.

Decal
A plastic, cloth, paper or ceramic substrate that has printed on it a pattern or image that can be moved to another surface on contact. Sometimes called a transfer.

Devoré
From the French for 'to devour', this printing technique uses a chemical paste that reacts with cellulosic fibres to burn them away when subjected to dry heat. Devoré is particularly effective with blended fabrics such as silk/viscose velvet where the cellulosic viscose velvet is burnt away to reveal the silk underneath, and also in conjunction with double-dyeing techniques.

Digital inkjet printing
A digitally driven print technology that sprays droplets of ink on to cloth through inkjet heads. It produces far less waste than conventional printing and provides flexibility in production output.

Drape
How a cloth hangs or falls.

Dye
Concentrate colour in powder form until mixed with the appropriate catalyst such as a print paste for use in printing interior and fashion fabrics.

Engineered print
A non-repeating design, often digitally generated and printed, conceived in relation to the shape and form of the product to which it will be applied.

Flocking
The application of suede or velvet motifs to a fabric surface through adhesive or electrostatic methods.

Foil
Metallic motif applied to a fabric surface using adhesive.

Hand screen-printing
See **Screen printing**.

Heat-transfer printing
A technique developed for printing on to synthetic and man-made fibres. Dyes are printed or painted on to the surface of a non-absorbent paper, which is then applied to the fabric and subjected to heat and pressure by a heat-transfer press or iron. This causes the dyes to vaporize and condense on to the surface of the fabric.

Laser cutting
A computer-directed cutting process using laser-beam technology that can cut intricate designs on a range of materials from fine silk to leather.

Mirroring
A symmetrical reflection of a motif, both subsequently repeated.

Nylon
A generic term for strong, lightweight, heat-resistant, synthetic man-made fibres composed of linear polyamide molecules.

Overprinting
The layering of two colours to make a third colour.

Pattern generation
The process of making a pattern in computer-aided design.

Pleat
A secured fold in a fabric that can be ironed to fall as a sharp crease or left to fall as a softer fold. A pleat sewn in place along its entire length is called a tuck.

Polyester
Any long-chain polymer containing 85 per cent esters in its main chain. Most synthetic polyesters are not biodegradable.

Protein fibres
Animal-based fibres such as wool and silk.

Repeat
The unit of a pattern that recurs to produce the whole.

Rhythm
The frequency, sequence or flow of a repeat pattern.

Rotary screen-printing
See **Screen printing**.

Sample
In the development of a printed fabric design, the production of samples enables the refinement of motif, pattern and colour. This refinement will be considered in relation to the fabric, printing method and other media to be used as well as the design's eventual context and use.

Screen printing
A technique in which a squeegee is used to push printing ink or dye through a screen mesh on to the cloth.

Stencil
In screen printing, the stencil is applied to the screen through which the ink or dye is passed using a squeegee to create the design on the cloth. Stencils can be produced either industrially as a film to be applied to a screen coated with photosensitive emulsion that is then exposed to ultra-violet light, or by digitally wax-spraying the design directly on to the screen.

Strike-off
A test piece of material printed to check the accuracy of pattern registration, pattern repeat and colour before approving the full manufacturing production of a design.

Sublimation printing
See **Heat-transfer printing.**

Substrate
The surface on to which a design has been printed.

Toile de Jouy
An illustrative style of printed design, sometimes narrative-based, usually printed in a single colour on a pale ground. It originated in the town of Jouy-en-Josas, near Paris.

Trompe l'œil
A realist painting and design technique often used in interiors to create the optical illusion of three-dimensionality on walls or ceilings.

Tulle
A lightweight, very fine netting, often starched, which can be made from a variety of yarns including silk and nylon.

Tweed
A rough-surfaced cloth made in plain or twill weave in two or three colours to create check or plaid patterns. Originally from Scotland.

Warp
Tensioned threads attached lengthwise or vertically to the loom to support the weft threads.

Weft
Horizontal filling threads in weaving that run from one edge to the other.

Credits

The author and publisher would like to thank the following for providing work and images for use in this book. In all cases every effort has been made to credit the copyright holders, but should there be any omissions or errors the publisher would be pleased to insert the appropriate acknowledgement in any subsequent editions of this book.

Ainsley Hillard
All artwork by Ainsley Hillard. p.183: Photograph by Robert Frith. pp.184-185: Photographs by Jason Ingram. pp.186-189: Photographs by Mojo Photography.

Anna Glover
All images courtesy of Anna Glover.

Arthur David
All images courtesy of Arthur David.

Astrid Sylwan for Marimekko
All artwork by Astrid Sylwan, © Marimekko. p.112: Photographs by Kristian Pohl. p.113: Photograph by Astrid Sylwan.

Basso & Brooke
All images courtesy of Basso & Brooke.

Brigitte Zieger
All images © Brigitte Zieger.

Cristian Zuzunaga
pp.199-200: Letterpress artwork by Cristian Zuzunaga, photographs by Mikolai Berg. p.201: Cristian Zuzunaga for Zuzunaga, photographs by David Casas. p.202: Digital print by Cristian Zuzunaga for Zuzunaga, photograph by Steve Nielsen. p.203: *Pixelated* fabric design by Cristian Zuzunaga, printed on to Trevira CS by Kvadrat, upholstering Springfield sofa by Patricia Urquiola for Moroso. pp.204-205: *Imaginatio* fabric design by Cristian Zuzunaga, printed on to Trevira CS by Kvadrat, upholstering Rue du jour sofa, NYA Meridienne 1, EOL Chair 1 and EOL Chair 2 by Christophe Delcourt, photographs by Pierre Even.

Deborah Bowness
Images courtesy of Deborah Bowness. p.120: Photograph by Claire Richardson. p.121 (top): Photograph by Nikki Divine. p.121 (bottom): Photograph © Andrew Meredith.

Dorte Agergaard
All images © Dorte Agergaard. Photographs by Åsmund Sollihøgda and Mathilde Schmidt.

Dries Van Noten
Images courtesy of Dries Van Noten. Photographs by Patrice Stable.

Eugène van Veldhoven
All images courtesy of Eugène van Veldhoven.

Francesco Simeti
pp.207 & 210: Courtesy of the artist and Francesca Minini, Milan. p.208: Courtesy of the artist and Wave Hill, Bronx, NY. Photographs by Daniel Mirer. p.209: © 2010 Francesco Simeti, Maharam under license.

p.211: Courtesy of the artist, Francesco Pantaleone Arte Contemporanea, Palermo, and Francesca Minini, Milan. p.212: © Francesco Simeti. MTA 18th Ave on the D line Bensonhurst Brooklyn. Commissioned and owned by MTA Arts for Transit and Urban Design, (bottom) photograph by Etienne Frossard. p.213: Courtesy of Francesco Simeti – Andrea Sala and Moroso, Udine.

Heidi Chisholm
All images courtesy of Heidi Chisholm, except p.38: Conceptualist: Kelly Vaagsland Wainwright, www.messymonkeyarts.com. Photograph by Charley Pollard.

Hussein Chalayan
pp.45 & 47: Courtesy of Chalayan. pp.48-51: catwalking.com.

Iris Maschek
All images courtesy of Iris Maschek. p.142: Photograph by Hannes Woidich. p.144: Photograph by Christian René Schulz. pp.145-147: Photographs by Constantin Meyer.

Issey Miyake
Images courtesy of Issey Mikaye, except pp.55 & 59: catwalking.com. p.58 (left): Gift of Alice A. Wolf. © 2014. Digital Image Museum Associates/LACMA/Art Resource NY/Scala, Florence. p.58 (right): Gift of Dale and Jonathan Gluckman. © 2014. Digital Image Museum Associates/LACMA/Art Resource NY/Scala, Florence.

Jakob Schlaepfer
All images © Jakob Schlaepfer.

Jim Isermann
pp.215, 220 (top left) & 221: Courtesy of the artist and Richard Telles Fine Art. pp.216-217 & 219: Courtesy of the artist and Corvi-Mora. p.218: Courtesy of the artist and Cirrus Gallery. p.220 (top right and bottom): Courtesy of the artist and Praz-Delavallade.

Katja Davar
All artwork © Katja Davar, courtesy of Galerie Kadel Willborn, Düsseldorf. pp.223 & 229: Photographs by Rainer Holz. pp.224 & 225: Animation stills by Edwin Bartnik. p.227: Photograph by Joerg Neumann. p.228: Photograph by Simon Vogel.

Liberty Art Fabrics
All images © Liberty Art Fabrics.

Maharam Digital Projects
p.149: © 2010 Paul Noble, Maharam under license. p.150 (top): Artwork © 2009 Harmen Liemburg, Maharam under license. Photograph by Lorenz Cugini, 2011, © Vitra. p.150 (bottom): © 2009 Harmen Liemburg, Maharam under license. p.151 (top left): Artwork © 2009 Karel Martens, Maharam under license. Photograph by Lorenz Cugini, 2011, © Vitra. p.151 (top right): © 2009 Karel Martens, Maharam under license. p.151 (bottom): © 2011 Markus Linnenbrink, Maharam under license. pp.152-153: © 2011 2x4 Inc., Maharam under license. p.154 (left): © 2010 Cecilia Edefalk, Maharam under license.

p.154 (right): Artwork © 2010 Cecilia Edefalk, Maharam under license. Photograph by Lorenz Cugini, 2011, © Vitra. p.155: Artwork © 2010 Sarah Morris, Maharam under license. Photograph by Lorenz Cugini, 2011, © Vitra.

Marly van Lipzig
pp.69, 71 & 72: Photographs by Marly van Lipzig. pp.70 & 73: Photographs by Bas van den Boom, model Yvette Serton at Cachetmodels, hair and make-up by Lisette Linssen van Lipzig at Francis Hair and Poetry. p.74: Photograph by Thierry DeLsaux at Shooting 1821, models Luca Wijnands (foreground) and Janine Stoffer (background). p.75: Photograph © Peter Stigter.

Peter Pilgrim
All images courtesy of Peter Pilgrim. p.240 (right): Kimono designed by Dianne Taylor, photograph by John Gulliver.

Peter Pilotto
All images courtesy of Peter Pilotto.

Prada
All images courtesy of Prada.

Richard Weston
All images courtesy of Richard Weston/ Weston Earth Images. p.252: Photograph by Peter Cook.

ROLLOUT
pp.157 & 158: Courtesy of ROLLOUT. p.159: Courtesy of ROLLOUT and Petra Reimann. p.160: Courtesy of ROLLOUT. p.161: Courtesy of Andrio Abero. p.162: Courtesy of ROLLOUT and David Palmer. p.163 (top): Courtesy of ROLLOUT. p.163 (bottom): Courtesy of Mike & Maaike.

Rupert Newman
All images © Rupert Newman.

Sally Greaves-Lord
All artwork © Sally Greaves-Lord, all photographs except pp.261 & 262 © Sally Greaves-Lord. pp.261-263: Sea Swim is supported by imove, Arts Council England, Lottery Funded. www.seaswim.co.uk. Photographs by John Wedgwood Clarke and Lara Goodband (pp.261 & 262) and Factor Imaginum (p.263). pp.264-265: Connections North is supported by Chrysalis Arts Development, Arts Council England, Lottery Funded. Photographs by Factor Imaginum. p.266: Bransholme Health Centre, Hull - lead artist: Linda Schwab, client: City Care – NHS Hull, architects: HLM. Photographs by Factor Imaginum. p.267: Celebrating Place is supported by Chrysalis Arts Development, Arts Council England, Lottery Funded, Y&NY Business Support Fund. Photographs by Factor Imaginum.

Timorous Beasties
All images courtesy of Timorous Beasties.

Todo Muta
All images courtesy of Todo Muta Studio.

Vivienne Westwood
All images courtesy of Vivienne Westwood.

Contacts

Ainsley Hillard
www.ainsleyhillard.com

Anna Glover
www.annaglover.co.uk

Arthur David
www.arthurdavid.ch

Astrid Sylwan
www.marimekko.com/marimekko/design/astrid-sylwan
Marimekko
www.marimekko.com

Basso & Brooke
www.bassoandbrooke.com

Brigitte Zieger
www.brigittezieger.com

Cristian Zuzunaga
www.cristianzuzunaga.com

Deborah Bowness
www.deborahbowness.com

Dorte Agergaard
www.dorteagergaard.dk

Dries Van Noten
www.driesvannoten.be

Eugène van Veldhoven
www.eugenevanveldhoven.nl

Francesco Simeti
www.francescosimeti.com

Heidi Chisholm
www.heidichisholm.com
Shine Shine
www.shineshine.co.za

Hussein Chalayan
husseinchalayan.com

Iris Maschek
www.irismaschek.com

Issey Miyake
www.isseymiyake.com

Jakob Schlaepfer
www.jakob-schlaepfer.ch

Jim Isermann
www.jimisermann.com

Katja Davar
www.katjadavar.com

Liberty Art Fabrics
www.liberty.co.uk/liberty-art-fabrics/article/fcp-content

Maharam Digital Projects
www.maharam.com/collections/maharam-digital-projects

Marly van Lipzig
www.marlyvanlipzig.com

Peter Pilgrim
ppilgrim@centencia.org

Peter Pilotto
www.peterpilotto.com

Prada
www.prada.com

Richard Weston
www.richardwestonstudio.com

ROLLOUT
www.rollout.ca

Rupert Newman
www.rupertnewman.com

Sally Greaves-Lord
www.sallygreaves-lord.com

Timorous Beasties
www.timorousbeasties.com

Todo Muta
www.todomuta.com

Vivienne Westwood
www.viviennewestwood.co.uk

Author's acknowledgements

Thanks to Falmouth University for its support and to all the artists and designers, design studios, manufacturers and businesses who contributed to this book. Thanks also to my publisher Laurence King and his team, especially Felicity Maunder, Helen Rochester, Simon Walsh and Sophie Wise, the book designer Shaz Madani, copy-editor Rosanna Lewis, and to my family and friends.